Planet Cake
KIDS

680 clever creations

Paris Cutler
with Anna Maria Roche

MURDOCH BOOKS

CONTENTS

INTRODUCTION

Get ready for a cake revolution!

The time has come to invite the next generation of cake-decorating superstars to pick up an icing smoother.

Cake decorating is not about being an expert or even a great baker. It's about being an artist and using your imagination to make amazing edible creations in sugar for your friends and family.

All you need are some of the skills outlined in this book, a few simple tools and some fondant icing. All of our cake toppers have been designed to be made by children aged eight years and over, and there is no need for any complex equipment.

The base cakes are designed to be made by adults or younger people of all skill levels.

My eight-year-old daughter, Estelle, is absolutely obsessed with making icing figurines, and has been asking me to write this book for a long time.

Estelle's figurines are often better than those made by adults. This is not because she has an innate talent — it's because once you learn a few simple figurine techniques, the only limit is your imagination, which comes alive in 3D.

Like most of us, I enjoyed baking and making sweets from a very young age. I also received a huge ego boost when I presented my delights to amazed and appreciative grown-ups.

This book introduces children to this wonderful craft, which truly gives so much joy, confidence and limitless possibilities to anyone who engages with it. I want to encourage adults and children to have fun learning and sharing new skills, being creative and spending time together.

For everyone else, this book is a great place to learn how to make simple yet effective icing figurines and fantastic cake designs.

The basic premise of this book is that children will be making the cake toppers, and grown-ups will be making the base cake.

Children are delightfully creative, so when I first started writing this book I had one very important question: what cake toppers do kids want to design and make?

I decided to do an experiment, which involved going to a school camp, where we were given access to large groups of 8–12-year-olds. Fighting the urge not to prompt the children with ideas, I decided to bring all our icing colours along — from pastels to primary colours — and gave them free access to choose what they wanted. We then gave a brief demonstration on how to attach a head to a body with spaghetti and left them to it. Interestingly, not a single pastel colour was used: the most popular colours for both boys and girls were lime green, bright pink and orange, red and black!

The children made the most wonderful cake toppers; the designs that were continually repeated included family, pets, junk food and crazy creatures, and it was these that influenced the designs in this book.

I also gave them four basic cake shapes contained in this book to decorate — and again I was in for a surprise, as they spent most of their time decorating the sides of the cake rather than the top.

At the end of the day, I turned to my right-hand decorator, Anna Maria, and we were both delightfully shocked. We should have had kids in our kitchen long before now!

HEY KIDS!

My daughter, Estelle, is eight years old and often works at Planet Cake making cake toppers. She also brings all her friends, and there are so many kids having fun with sugar at our shop, I decided to write this book so that *you too* can become a Cake Artist.

Being a Cake Artist is one of the best jobs you could ever have. You get to use your imagination and create your own cake topper designs. You get to work with other creative people — other kids, grown-ups, or even Mum or Dad. And you basically just play all day sculpting different characters out of sugar.

Does this sound like fun so far? I haven't told you the best bit yet! After you have made your incredible edible creations and placed them on an amazing cake, you get to give the cake to someone special. It's a really special feeling to give someone a magical cake. It makes you feel very proud of yourself — and then you can't wait to make the next one!

I could have written this book just for kids, but I've included grown-ups as well, because it's always fun to work on a cake together, and the cake will be even better than if you worked on your own. Grown-ups need kids' help because kids often have better imaginations — which is why *you* should make the cake toppers. However, the cake base may be a trickier job, and grown-ups would probably be more experienced with this.

Perhaps there are some really talented kids who would like to make both the toppers and the cake. That would be fantastic, but these projects are really fun to share.

After all, cakes are all about making people happy!

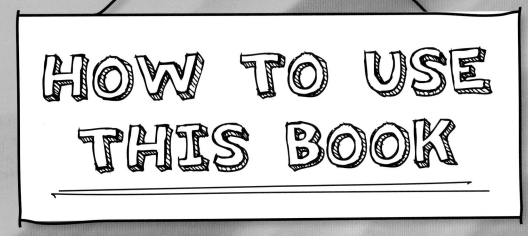

HOW TO USE THIS BOOK

HOW TO USE THIS BOOK

Before we get to the fun bit — creating a beautiful cake base and topping it with hand-crafted figurines! — it's a good idea to have a look through the decorating basics explained in chapter 6, especially if you're new to cake decorating.

In particular, 'Tricks of the trade' (page 164) shares important secrets about planning and preparation so everything proceeds smoothly. Our 'Tools of the trade' section (page 168) gives a photographic reference for stocking your kitchen, and there's also a Glossary (page 170) explaining some terms and items you may not be familiar with if you're new to this business of being a Cake Artist.

You'll also find some great recipes for making your own icings (page 174), to use on the fabulous cakes in chapter 3 (page 24). These are the same cakes that we use at Planet Cake, so we know the recipes work well, the cakes are firm enough to give a good basis for decorating, and they also store well.

Then it's time to unleash your creativity. Flick through this chapter and you'll see just some of the possibilities for topping different basic cake designs with a whole range of figurine families. You can literally mix and match your preferred cake base with your preferred figurine or figurines, to suit a particular person or certain occasion.

See which combinations appeal to the creative team, then just hop to it.

Once you've had a look at some nifty techniques to get great effects with icing (page 178), it's time for the kids to turn Cake Artist and conjure up some figurines from the 'Cake toppers' chapter (page 90 onwards). These figurines need some time to dry, so it's a good idea to get kids working on these well ahead of final decorating time.

The next step is to cut and shape your choice of baked cake, following the techniques in chapter 3 (page 28 onwards), before assembling your whole mix-and-match masterpiece, using one of the fun cake designs covered in chapter 4. Each cake design lists the particular materials and equipment you'll need, and the steps you need to take.

Rest assured this isn't as complicated as it may sound — once you get the hang of it and see the finished cake in all its glory, you'll find the whole process immensely rewarding.

You probably won't need it, but there's also a quick section on 'Trouble-shooting' at the back of the book (page 184), just in case of little mishaps. So let's have some fun!

MIX AND MATCH... MAKE IT YOUR OWN

It is important to choose your figurines first, as they will be the focus of the cake, and choose the cake design second, as the cake is really a 'stage' for the figurines.

The figurines in this book are based on different 'families' of creatures, but I encourage you to mix them up — it's exciting to see a monster with a dog, or a dragon with a superhero.

The best thing about the cake toppers is that you are not at all limited. Once you learn that they are only as complex as dry spaghetti and icing, the design possibilities are literally endless. So feel free to mix up your cake designs and characters, and also to improvise on these designs.

BEACH

Hip hop dudes
Little nipper
lifesavers
Superhero family

Snow-surfing
penguins
Sporty dogs

WIZARD BOOK

Superhero family
Baby dragons
Fat rats
Mrs Zucker's bits & pieces

CARTOON CAKE

Fat rats
Mr Donut & friends
Softie bears
Superhero family
Angel babies
Pig & Pepper

COOKING POT

Fat rats
Little nipper lifesavers
Baby dragons
Superhero family
Hip hop dudes
Ninja rabbits

CANDY FLOSS CLOUDS

Softie bears
Pig & Pepper
Sporty dogs
Baby angels
Mr Donut & friends
Snow-surfing penguins
Baby dragons

VIDEO GAME

Video nuts
The Stompers
Snow-Surfing penguins

MARTIAL ARTS RING

Ninja rabbits
Hip hop dudes
Sporty dogs
The Stompers
Superhero family

MAN IN THE MOON

Little nipper lifesavers
Pig & Pepper
Superhero family
Ninja rabbits

GRAVEYARD

Mrs Zucker's bits & pieces
The Stompers
Video nuts

GRAFFITI WALL

Superhero family

Video nuts

The Stompers

Baby dragons

Little nipper lifesavers

Hip hop dudes

SNOW CAP

Any figurines

ALL ABOUT CAKES

CAKE RECIPES

Vanilla buttercake

Preparation: 15 minutes
Cooking: 50 minutes + cooling
Makes one 22 cm (9 in) round cake or
one 20 cm (8 in) square cake

250 g (9 oz/1⅔ cups) self-raising flour
75 g (2½ oz/½ cup) plain (all-purpose) flour
220 g (7¾ oz/1 cup) caster (superfine) sugar
185 g (6½ oz) unsalted butter, softened
4 eggs, at room temperature
125 ml (4 fl oz/½ cup) milk
1 teaspoon vanilla extract

1 Preheat the oven to 180°C (350°F/Gas 4).
  Grease your cake tin and line the base
  and side with baking paper.
2 Sift the flours into a large bowl. Add the
  sugar, butter, eggs, milk and vanilla. Using
  electric beaters, beat on low speed until
  combined. Increase the speed to medium
  and beat for 2–3 minutes, or until the
  mixture is well combined and pale.
3 Spoon the mixture into the cake tin, then
  smooth the surface with the back of the
  spoon. Bake on the centre rack of the
  oven for 45–50 minutes, or until a skewer
  inserted into the centre of the cake
  comes out clean.
4 Leave the cake in the tin for 5 minutes,
  before turning out onto a wire rack to
  cool completely.

STORAGE
This cake will keep in an airtight container
for up to 3 days. It can be frozen, without
decoration, for up to 2 months. Wrap tightly
in plastic wrap, then place in a freezer bag
and seal. It's a good idea to write the date
on the bag.

VARIATION
To make a marbled cake, divide the cake
mixture among three bowls. Tint one bowl
with a few drops of pink food colouring,
and another bowl with 2 tablespoons
unsweetened cocoa powder. Leave the
third bowl plain. Alternately drop spoonfuls
of each mixture into the prepared cake
tin, then use a skewer to lightly swirl the
mixtures together. Bake as directed above.

Chocolate mud cake

Preparation: 20 minutes
Cooking: 1 hour 55 minutes + cooling
Makes one 22 cm (9 in) round cake or
one 20 cm (8 in) square cake

225 g (8 oz) butter
225 g (8 oz) dark chocolate, chopped
480 g (1 lb 1 oz/2¼ cups) caster (superfine)
  sugar
15 g (½ oz/¼ cup) coffee granules
3 eggs, lightly beaten
150 g (5½ oz/1 cup) self-raising flour, sifted
150 g (5½ oz/1 cup) plain (all-purpose)
  flour, sifted
40 g (1½ oz/⅓ cup) unsweetened cocoa powder

1 Preheat the oven to 160°C (315°F/Gas 2–3). Grease your cake tin and line the base and side with baking paper.

2 Combine the butter, chocolate, sugar and coffee in a large saucepan with 250 ml (9 fl oz/1 cup) hot water. Stir over low heat until smooth. Transfer to a large bowl and leave to cool for 15 minutes.

3 Whisk the eggs into the chocolate mixture, then whisk in the sifted flours and cocoa until the mixture is smooth.

4 Pour the mixture into the cake tin and bake for 1 hour 45 minutes. Test the centre with a skewer — it may be slightly wet. If the top looks raw, bake for another 5–10 minutes, then remove from the oven.

5 Leave the cake in the tin for 5 minutes, before turning out onto a wire rack to cool completely.

STORAGE

This cake can be stored in an airtight container in the refrigerator for up to 3 weeks, or in a cool, dry place for up to 1 week. It can be frozen, without decoration, for up to 2 months. Wrap tightly in plastic wrap, then place in a freezer bag and seal. It's a good idea to write the date on the bag.

Red velvet cake

Preparation: 20 minutes
Cooking: 50 minutes + cooling
Makes one 22 cm (9 in) round cake or one 20 cm (8 in) square cake

185 g (6½ oz) unsalted butter, softened
275 g (9¾ oz/1¼ cups) caster (superfine) sugar
3 eggs
300 g (10½ oz/2 cups) self-raising flour
55 g (2 oz/½ cup) unsweetened cocoa powder
1 teaspoon bicarbonate of soda (baking soda)
250 ml (9 fl oz/1 cup) buttermilk
2 teaspoons white vinegar
2 teaspoons liquid red food colouring

1 Preheat the oven to 180°C (350°F/Gas 4). Grease your cake tin and line the base and side with baking paper.

2 Cream the butter and sugar in a small bowl using electric beaters until light and fluffy. Add the eggs one at a time, beating thoroughly after each addition. Transfer to a large bowl.

3 Sift the flour, cocoa and bicarbonate of soda into a bowl. Combine the buttermilk, vinegar and food colouring. Using a large metal spoon, fold the flour mixture into the butter mixture alternately with the buttermilk mixture. Stir until just combined and almost smooth.

4 Spoon the mixture into the cake tin and smooth the surface with the back of the spoon. Bake for 45–50 minutes, or until a skewer inserted into the centre of the cake comes out clean.

5 Leave the cake in the tin for 10 minutes, before turning out onto a wire rack to cool completely.

STORAGE

This cake will keep in an airtight container for up to 3 days. It can be frozen, without decoration, for up to 2 months. Wrap tightly in plastic wrap, then place in a freezer bag and seal. It's a good idea to write the date on the bag.

Dairy-free, egg-free banana cake

Due to the density of this cake, it might sink slightly in the centre during baking. This slight dip can be filled with ganache or buttercream when covering your cake.

Preparation: 20 minutes
Cooking: 1 hour + cooling
Makes one 22 cm (9 in) round cake or one 20 cm (8 in) square cake

185 g (6½ oz) dairy-free spread
220 g (7¾ oz/1 cup firmly packed) brown sugar
1 teaspoon vanilla extract
360 g (12¾ oz/1½ cups) mashed banana (about 3 large bananas)
45 g (1½ oz/½ cup) desiccated coconut
300 g (10½ oz/2 cups) self-raising flour, sifted
1 teaspoon bicarbonate of soda (baking soda)
1 teaspoon mixed spice (all spice)
1 teaspoon ground cinnamon

1 Preheat the oven to 180°C (350°F/Gas 4). Grease your cake tin and line the base and side with baking paper.

2 Cream the dairy-free spread, sugar and vanilla in a small bowl using electric beaters for 3–4 minutes, or until light and fluffy. Transfer to a large bowl.

3 Using a large metal spoon, fold in the mashed banana and coconut, then the sifted flour, bicarbonate of soda and spices. Stir until just combined and almost smooth.

4 Spoon the mixture into the tin and smooth the surface with the back of the spoon. Bake for 1 hour, or until a skewer inserted into the centre of the cake comes out clean.

5 Leave the cake in the tin for 10 minutes, before turning out onto a wire rack to cool completely.

VARIATION

For a regular banana cake, replace the dairy-free spread with butter, and beat 3 eggs into the creamed butter and sugar mixture. Delete the coconut and increase the flour by 35 g (1¼ oz/¼ cup). Bake as directed above.

STORAGE

This cake will keep in an airtight container for up to 4 days. It can be frozen, without decoration, for up to 2 months. Wrap tightly in plastic wrap, then place in a freezer bag and seal. It's a good idea to write the date on the bag.

Gluten-free buttercake

Due to the lack of gluten in this cake, it might sink slightly in the centre during baking. This slight dip can be filled with ganache or buttercream when covering your cake.

Preparation: 15 minutes
Cooking: 50 minutes + cooling
Makes one 22 cm (9 in) round cake or one 20 cm (8 in) square cake

250 g (9 oz/1⅔ cups) gluten-free
   self-raising flour
220 g (7¾ oz/1 cup) caster
   (superfine) sugar
185 g (6½ oz) unsalted butter,
   softened
80 ml (2½ fl oz/⅓ cup) milk
4 eggs, at room temperature
1 teaspoon vanilla extract

1 Preheat the oven to 180°C (350°F/Gas 4). Grease your cake tin and line the base and side with baking paper.
2 Sift the flour and 55 g (2 oz/¼ cup) of the sugar into a bowl. Beat the butter in a small bowl using electric beaters for 4–5 minutes, or until pale and creamy. Gradually beat in the flour and sugar mixture and the milk until just combined. Transfer to a large bowl.
3 Using an electric mixer with a whisk attachment, whisk the eggs, vanilla and remaining sugar in a bowl for about 5–6 minutes, or until very thick and pale and tripled in volume. Using a spatula or large metal spoon, stir half the egg mixture into the flour mixture. Fold in the remaining egg mixture until just combined.
4 Spoon the mixture into the cake tin and smooth the surface with the back of the spoon. Bake on the centre rack of the oven for 40–50 minutes, or until a skewer inserted into the centre of the cake comes out clean.
5 Leave the cake in the tin for 10 minutes, before turning out onto a wire rack to cool completely.

STORAGE

This cake will keep in an airtight container for up to 3 days. It can be frozen, without decoration, for up to 2 months. Wrap tightly in plastic wrap, then place in a freezer bag and seal. It's a good idea to write the date on the bag.

CAKE TECHNIQUES

Ganaching

Chocolate ganache — a melted mixture of chocolate and cream — will not only make your cake taste better and keep it moist, but will also give you a perfect surface for icing. At Planet Cake we use ganache as a sort of edible 'putty' to fill in all the crevices and holes in the cake, and create an even surface.

Once the ganache has set hard and is perfectly smooth, it presents a firm and perfect surface for covering with thin icing — rather than the thick, unpalatable icing that some decorators use to hide imperfections in the cake.

Follow the recipe for making ganache (page 174) and allow it to set overnight. If the ganache is too hard when you are ready to use it, heat it in the microwave on medium power (50%) in short bursts, until it reaches the consistency of smooth peanut butter. If you don't have a microwave, put the ganache in a saucepan and stir it over low heat, making sure you don't burn it.

Alternatively, you could use a layer of buttercream (pages 176–177) under your fondant icing, but it will not set as firm as ganache, and so will not give you the same perfect finish.

Ganaching a round cake

1 Slice your cake horizontally into three even layers

Trim the dome from the top of the cake to get a flat surface. Put the cake on a turntable and place one hand on top of the cake (never keep your hand on the side as the knife could slip). Hold a long serrated knife in the other hand, making sure to keep the knife level.

Mark the cutting lines on the cake by scoring the side; each layer should be about 2.5 cm (1 in) thick (photo 1).

Rotate the cake and cut towards the centre using a sawing action, gradually cutting deeper. Continue turning and cutting deeper every round, making sure to keep the knife at the same horizontal level.

Repeat this step one more time to cut another layer.

Tip: If your cake is cracked or uneven on the top, swap the middle layer with the top layer so that you can hide it inside the cake.

2 Brush with syrup

For the next step you'll need some syrup (page 176). Place the three layers of cake on your work surface, then brush each fairly liberally with syrup (photo 2).

3 Fill the cake with ganache

Use a palette knife to spread some ganache on a cake board the same size as the cake — for example, a 20 cm (8 in) cake would be placed on a 20 cm (8 in) board. We refer to this board as the set-up or temp board.

Place the bottom cake layer on your set-up or temp board. Spread ganache over the bottom cake layer, to about 1 cm (½ in) thick, then sandwich the next layer on top. Cover with more ganache (photo 3), then sandwich the third layer on top.

Do not spread ganache on the top of the cake at this point.

Tip: Having a set-up or temp board is very important when ganaching, as it allows you to make a big mess — and, most importantly, serves as a guide for measuring the filling. Cakes shrink during the baking process, and placing the cake on the same size cake board lets you see how much ganache to apply to bring the cake back to the correct size.

4 Apply ganache to the side

Place the set-up board on your display board, then place it back on the turntable. Using a palette knife, apply ganache all around the side of the cake, out to the edge of the set-up board. Do not spread ganache on the top of the cake yet.

5 Scrape off the excess ganache

Put one hand on top of the cake and slowly run a plastic scraper around the side of the cake. Make sure you hold the scraper straight on the edge of the set-up board. Using the turntable, keep turning until your cake has a perfectly vertical edge and all the gaps are filled (photo 4, page 30).

Tip: Your goal is to fill the side of the cake until it meets the rim of the set-up board. This may take some time, and will require more ganache than you envisage. Make sure you have a perfect right-angle — if the filling bulges out, there will be a lump on your cake. Alternatively, if there is not enough ganache and the side is not flat, you will have ridges.

6 Apply ganache to the top

Use a small palette knife to smear the excess ganache over the edge of the cake and onto the top, then level the top (photo 5). Use more ganache on the top if necessary.

Let it set (preferably overnight), or freeze for a maximum of 10 minutes.

7 Hot-knife the cake

To achieve a perfect result, you'll need a jug of boiling water and a long knife to run over the cake to make sure the edge is perfect.

Take a large palette knife and let it stand in the hot water for a few seconds. (Alternatively you can use the non-serrated back edge of a bread knife.)

Hold the knife at both ends and glide it over the surface of the cake, making sure to apply even pressure along the whole length of the knife. If the ganache is uneven, apply more to level the cake.

Run the plastic scraper once more around the side of the cake. Let the cake set again and, when it is hard, use a hot knife to cut the overhang off the top edge (photo 6).

Clean your display board and leave the cake until the ganache has set hard — preferably overnight — before you cover it.

Ganaching a square cake

Follow the same guidelines as for the round cake to the end of step 3. The same method applies to rectangular cakes.

1 Ganache and smooth

Put the set-up board on your display board. Using a palette knife, apply the ganache thickly to the sides (about 2 cm/¾ in), to build up the cake. Scrape off the excess with a scraper and apply more ganache until you have very sharp edges. Smooth the ganache (photo 1). Let the ganache set until it is firm to the touch (1–2 hours).

Apply ganache on the top, smooth, and again allow to set — preferably overnight.

2 Hot-knife the cake

Hot-knife the ganache, starting at one side. Glide over the surface, making sure to apply even pressure along the length of the knife (photo 2), scraping off any excess ganache.

Run the plastic scraper once more around the sides, keeping the corners sharp.

Frosting a cake with buttercream

1 Prepare the cake

With your serrated knife, trim the top of the cake to create an even surface. Place the cake on a stand or plate. To keep it neat, tuck strips of baking paper underneath the cake, before you begin frosting.

2 Crumb-coat the cake

Spread a thin layer of buttercream over the cake to seal in the crumbs (this is called 'crumb-coating').

Chill for about 30 minutes, before applying the final coat of buttercream. This will help stop crumbs from working their way into the layer of frosting.

3 Frosting

Take your palette knife and mound all of your frosting on top of the cake. Now start to work the frosting down the sides of the cake — you can make it as rough or smooth as you like. Carefully remove the strips of baking paper before serving the cake.

4 Storing

If you are covering your cake with vanilla buttercream (page 177), it can be stored at room temperature (no higher than 20°C/68°F) for up to 2 days.

If you are using the Italian buttercream (page 176), your cake must be stored in the refrigerator; it will keep for 2–3 days.

If you don't have a cake box to store your cake in, try using a large inverted bowl or a foil 'tent' that you make yourself to cover your cake.

If you have to cover a frosted cake with plastic wrap, first stick toothpicks evenly all over the top of the cake. The plastic wrap will rest on the toothpick tops, instead of the frosting.

Covering a round cake with fondant

Make sure your cake is smoothly ganached and allowed to set before you cover it with icing. The more perfectly the cake is ganached, the better the final result will be. Round cakes are the easiest to cover.

1 Prepare the cake and icing

Wipe your work surface clean and make sure it is dry. Measure the cake (side and top surface). Brush the cake all over with a little syrup (page 176); this helps the fondant stick to the cake (photo 1).

Place the cake, still on its display board, on a non-slip mat or a moist tea towel (dish towel), so it doesn't slip while you are working on it.

Knead your fondant icing (and colour it, if you wish — see pages 178–179) to a smooth, pliable dough. During kneading,

you can use a sprinkling of cornflour (cornstarch) if the dough sticks to the work surface.

Tip: Kneading icing is not like kneading dough. If you keep pummelling, it will stick to the board and become unmanageable. Treat your icing a bit like Play-Doh: keep folding it in until it is smooth and warm to use, but doesn't stick to the work surface.

2 Flatten and roll the icing

Making sure your icing is smooth, flatten your ball of icing with the palm of your hand to about 4 cm (1½ in) thick (photo 2).

Dust some cornflour on your work surface. Roll out the icing with a rolling pin, starting from the centre and rolling about six times in one direction.

Turn the icing, then repeat the process. If your work surface gets sticky, sprinkle it with a bit more cornflour — but never use cornflour on top of the icing.

Keep on rolling and turning until your icing is about 3–5 mm (⅛–¼ in) thick. The icing needs to be larger than the total cake measurement.

Tip: Turning the icing will ensure it will always be a square, which will make covering a round or square cake much easier.

3 Lift the icing over the cake

Pick up the icing by rolling it onto a rolling pin. Use a dry pastry brush to remove any excess cornflour — this is particularly important if you use a dark-coloured icing.

Lift up the rolling pin with the icing and unroll it over the cake, starting from the base of the cake (photo 3).

4 Secure the edges

Quickly run your hand over the top surface of the cake to make sure there are no air bubbles.

Secure the edges by running the palm of your hand along the top edge and side of the cake (photo 4).

5 Smooth the icing

Press the icing gently against the side, slowly working around the cake. Gently pull the icing away from the bottom of the cake, before smoothing it down (photo 5, page 34).

6 Use icing smoothers

Once the whole cake is covered, gently press the icing against the side and base of the cake using icing smoothers, to make a cutting line (photo 6, page 34).

7 Trim the icing

Trim the icing around the base with a knife or pizza wheel (photo 7, page 34).

Tip: Do not trim your icing too close to the base of your cake, as icing can shrink once it has been cut, and you could be left with

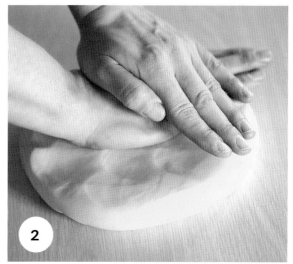

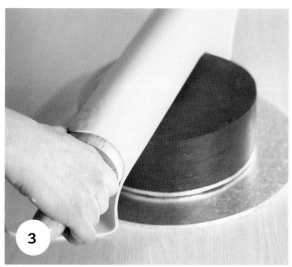

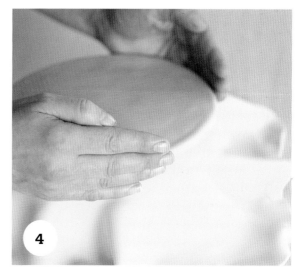

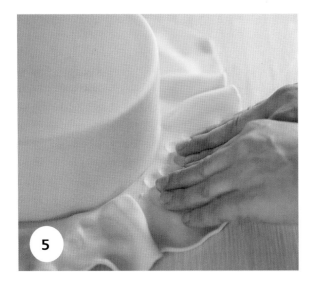

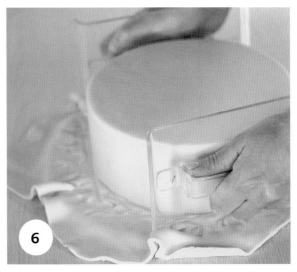

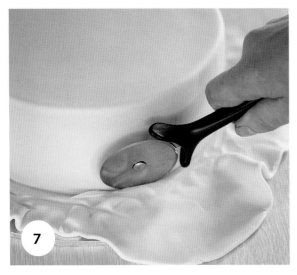

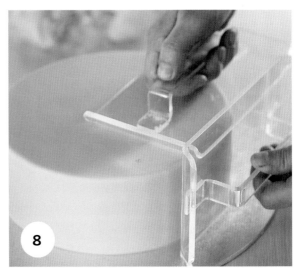

a gap. If this does happen, adjust your design and hide the gap by placing a thin roll or 'rope' of leftover icing around the base of the cake.

8 Use your smoothers

Run your smoother along the side of the cake. I use two smoothers for this job — the one in the left hand is running back and forth, and the one in the right hand is pressed against the cake to make a sharp edge.

Next, hold one smoother on the side of the cake and the other one on the top. Using the same amount of pressure on each, press them together and run all along the side of the cake to give a sharp edge (photo 8).

Glide your hand along the cake feeling for air bubbles. If there are any, poke a small pin into the bubble and gently release the air using dry fingers (see page 185).

Go over the cake with your smoother or flexi-scraper to buff and polish the icing.

Covering a square cake with fondant

Use the same guidelines as for the round cake on page 32, until the end of step 3. As soon as the icing is on the cake, secure the corners immediately, as shown below.

1 Secure the corners
Working on both sides of each corner, run both hands down along each corner, pressing the icing onto the cake (photo 1).

2 Push the icing down
Push the icing right down the corners with your fingers by running them up and down along the edges (photo 2).

3 Pull and smooth the sides
Gently pull the icing away from the sides with one hand and smooth it down with the other hand. Then run your hands up again to avoid tears or cracks in the icing.
   Trim all around the base using a small knife or pizza wheel.

4 Smooth the icing
Run your icing smoother around the cake. Use two flexi-scrapers and run them towards each other at the corners to achieve a sharp edge (photo 3).

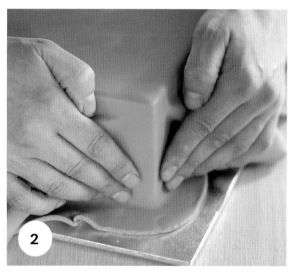

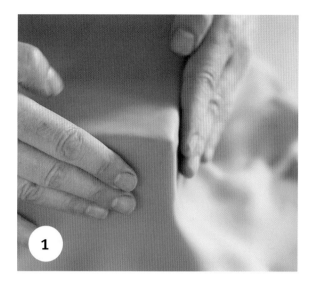

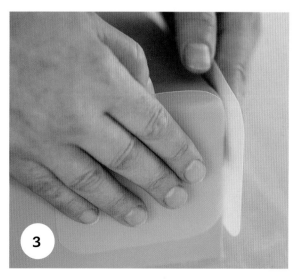

Ganaching a wall cake

Here's how to create and ganache a wall cake, using a 20 cm (8 in) square cake.

1 Make a wall

Make a set-up or temp board by sawing a normal 20 cm (8 in) board in half.

Follow the instructions on page 28 to slice the cake horizontally into three even layers. Brush each layer fairly liberally with syrup.

Spread ganache over one cake layer, to about 1 cm (½ in) thick, then sandwich the next layer on top. Cover with more ganache, then sandwich the third layer on top.

Cut your cake in half down the middle (photo 1), to give two rectangular cakes, each 10 x 20 cm (4 x 8 in). Place one cake half on the set-up board, cover the top with ganache, then place the other cake on top.

2 Ganache the sides and top

Place the set-up board on a display board, then onto a turntable. With a palette knife, spread ganache over the top of the cake to seal the crumbs. Ganache the sides.

3 Smooth the sides and top

Slowly run a 90° plastic scraper along all sides, holding the scraper straight on the board, while slowly turning the turntable.

Use a small palette knife to smear excess ganache from the sides, over the edge. Straighten the top, using more ganache if needed. Let the ganache set for a few hours.

4 Hot-knife the cake

Dip a large palette knife in hot water for a few seconds. (Alternatively you can use the non-serrated back edge of a bread knife.)

Hold the knife at both ends and glide it over the top of the cake, making sure to apply even pressure to the knife (photo 2).

If the ganache is uneven, apply more ganache to level the cake. Run your plastic scraper once more around each side of the cake.

Allow the ganache to set once again.

5 Trim the overhang

Cut the overhang off the top edge. Clean the display board, then allow the cake to sit until the ganache has set hard — preferably overnight — before you decorate it.

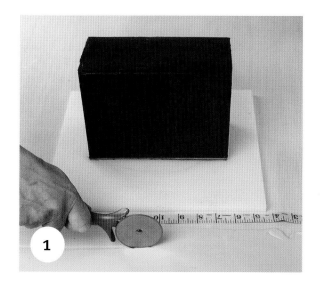

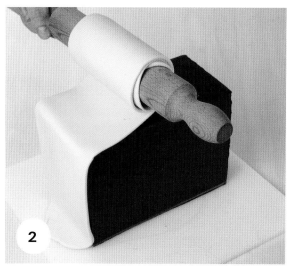

Covering a wall cake with fondant

Make sure your cake is ganached and the ganache has set before you attempt to cover your cake. The better the ganache preparation, the better your cake will look.

1 Prepare the cake and icing

Wipe your work surface clean and make sure it is dry. Measure the cake (side and top surface). Brush the cake all over with a little syrup (page 176); this helps the fondant stick to the cake.

Place the display board on a non-slip mat or moist tea towel (dish towel) so the cake doesn't slip while you are working on it.

Knead your fondant icing (and colour it, if you wish — see pages 178–179) to a smooth, pliable dough. During kneading, you can use a sprinkle of cornflour (cornstarch) if the dough sticks to the work surface.

Tip: Kneading icing is not like kneading dough. If you keep pummelling, it will stick to the board and become unmanageable. Treat your icing a bit like Play-Doh: keep folding it in until it is smooth and warm to use, but doesn't stick to the bench.

2 Flatten and roll the icing

Making sure your icing is smooth, flatten your ball of icing with the palm of your hand to about 4 cm (1½ in) thick.

Dust some cornflour on your work surface. Roll out the icing with a rolling pin, starting from the centre and rolling about six times in one direction.

Turn the icing, then repeat the process. If your work surface gets sticky, sprinkle it with a bit more cornflour — but never use cornflour on top of the icing.

Using the measurements of the cake, roll out a strip of icing long enough and wide enough to cover the top of the cake and the two skinny sides in one piece. Add 5 cm (2 in) to both the length and width. Keep on rolling and turning until your icing is about 3–5 mm (⅛–¼ in) thick, then cut out the strip of icing you require (photo 1, page 37).

Tip: Turning the icing will ensure it will always be a square, which will make covering the cake much easier.

3 Lift the icing over the cake

Pick up the icing by rolling it onto a rolling pin. Use a dry pastry brush to remove any excess cornflour — this is particularly important if you use a dark-coloured icing.

Lift up the rolling pin with the icing and unroll it over the cake, starting with one of the skinny sides and rolling it over the top of the cake (photo 2, page 37).

4 Secure the edges

Quickly run your hand over the top surface to make sure there are no air bubbles.

Secure the edges by running the palm of your hand along the top edge and side of the cake.

5 Trim the icing

Using a sharp knife, trim all the excess icing.

Tip: Do not trim your icing too close to the base of your cake, as icing can shrink once it has been cut, and you could be left with a gap. If this does happen, adjust your design and hide the gap by placing a thin roll or 'rope' of leftover icing around the base of the cake.

6 Hone the edges

Use two flexi-scrapers and work them against each other to achieve a sharp edge.

7 Cover the sides

Now that the top and skinny sides of the cake are covered, it's time to cover the two large sides of your wall. Again measure the icing you will require, roll your icing out and cut two pieces.

Brush the sides of your cake with syrup. Place a piece of icing flush against the bottom of the cake, then work the icing up by flipping it up and sticking it on.

Repeat the same process of securing the icing, smoothing and checking for air bubbles, as you did with the skinny sides.

8 Use your smoothers

Run your smoother along the side of the cake. I use two smoothers to do this job — the one in the left hand is running back and forth, and the one in the right hand is pressed against the cake to make a sharp edge.

Next, hold one smoother on the side of the cake and the other one on the top. Using the same amount of pressure on each, press them together and run all along the side of the cake to give a sharp edge.

Glide your hand along the cake feeling for air bubbles. If there are any, poke a small pin into the bubble and gently release the air using dry fingers (see page 185).

Go over the cake with your smoother or flexi-scraper to buff and polish the icing.

Ganaching a dome cake

All the dome cakes in this book are made from a 22 cm (9 in) round cake. To set it up you'll need a 25 cm (9 in) round set-up or temp board, as well as a 35 cm (14 in) display board. Layering the dome cake with ganache ensures it is yummy to eat, and also makes shaping the cake easier.

1 Slice your cake horizontally into three even layers

Put the cake on a turntable and place one hand on top of the cake (never keep your hand on the side as the knife could slip). Hold a long serrated knife in the other hand, making sure to keep the knife level.

Mark the cutting lines on the cake by scoring the side; each layer should be about 2.5 cm (1 in) thick. Rotate the cake and cut towards the centre with a sawing action, gradually cutting deeper.

Continue turning and cutting deeper every round, making sure to keep the knife at the same horizontal level.

Repeat this one more time to cut another layer (photo 1).

2 Brush with syrup

Place the three layers of cake on your work surface, and brush each fairly liberally with syrup (page 176).

3 Fill the cake with ganache

Use a palette knife to spread some ganache on your 25 cm (10 in) set-up board. Place the bottom cake layer on the set-up board.

Spread ganache over the bottom layer of the cake, to about 1 cm (½ in) thick, then

sandwich the next layer on top. Cover the second cake layer with more ganache, then sandwich the third layer on top.

Do not cover the top of the cake with ganache at this point.

Tip: Having a set-up or temp board is very important when ganaching, as it allows you to make a big mess.

4 Create your dome

Place the set-up board on a display board.

With your set-up board as a guide, cut your cake into a dome shape (photo 2, page 39), shaving the cake from the top, but keeping the bottom edge intact. Keep the shaved-off bits of cake handy.

The next step will be messy and gooey, so don't be alarmed if your cake ends up being made of many pieces. After it receives its final layer of ganache it will be delicious and look perfect!

Use your ganache as a glue to stick the shaved-off pieces back onto the cake (photo 3, page 39). The idea is to amass enough cake to carve or sculpt your shape. (It will look a far cry from a dome before it is rough ganached and then hot-knifed.)

Leave the ganache to set for a few hours.

5 Hot-knife the cake

Dip a palette knife in hot water. Smooth the ganache, gliding the palette knife over the top of the cake and down the side, making sure to apply even pressure to the knife. If the ganache is uneven, apply more ganache to level the cake.

Clean the display board, then let the cake sit until the ganache has set hard — preferably overnight — before decorating.

Covering a dome cake with fondant

All the same principles apply with a domed cake as they do with a round or square cake. Make sure your cake is ganached and the ganache has set before you cover your cake. The better the ganache preparation, the better your cake will look.

1 Prepare the cake and icing

Wipe your work surface clean and make sure it is dry. Measure the cake (side and top surface). Brush the cake all over with a little syrup (page 176); this helps the fondant stick to the cake.

Place the display board on a non-slip mat or a moist tea towel (dish towel) so it doesn't slip while you are working on it.

Knead your fondant icing (and colour it, if you wish — see pages 178–179) to a smooth, pliable dough. During kneading, you can use a sprinkle of cornflour (cornstarch) if the dough sticks to the work surface.

Tip: Kneading icing is not like kneading dough. If you keep pummelling, it will stick to the board and become unmanageable. Treat your icing a bit like Play-Doh: keep folding it in until it is smooth and warm to use, but doesn't stick to the bench.

2 Flatten and roll the icing

Making sure your icing is smooth, flatten your ball of icing with the palm of your hand to about 4 cm (1½ in) thick.

Dust some cornflour on your work surface. Roll out the icing with a rolling pin, starting from the centre and rolling about six times in one direction.

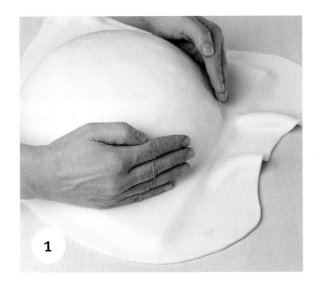

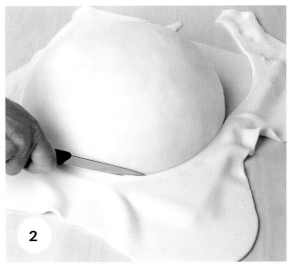

Turn the icing, then repeat the process. If your work surface gets sticky, sprinkle it with a bit more cornflour — but never use cornflour on top of the icing. Keep on rolling and turning until your icing is about 3–5 mm (⅛–¼ in) thick. The icing needs to be larger than the total cake measurement.

Tip: Turning the icing will ensure it will always be a square, which will make covering the cake much easier.

3 Lift the icing over the cake

Pick up the icing by rolling it onto a rolling pin. Use a dry pastry brush to remove any excess cornflour — this is particularly important if you use a dark-coloured icing.
Lift up the rolling pin with the icing and unroll it over the cake.

4 Secure the icing

Quickly run your hand over the top surface to make sure there are no air bubbles. Smooth out any creases and unusual shapes with your hands and fingers. Secure the edges of the cake by running the palm

of your hand along the side of the cake, holding your hand in the 'karate chop' position (photo 1).

5 Trim the icing

Once the whole cake is covered, use the back of a sharp knife to gently press the icing against the side and base of the cake. Tuck it under to make a cutting line, then trim the icing with the knife (photo 2).

Tip: Do not trim your icing too close to the base of your cake: icing can shrink once it has been cut and you may be left with a gap. If this does happen, adjust your design and hide the gap by placing a thin roll or 'rope' of leftover icing around the base of the cake.

6 Buff and polish the icing

Using your magical flexi-scraper, buff and polish the icing against the cake, creating a more defined shape. The longer you spend doing this, the better the shape will look. Make sure every air bubble is eliminated (see page 185), gently working the icing with your hands and the flexi-scraper.

WIZARD BOOK

This cake has so many fantastically different design options. It could also become a graduation cake, a cookbook, a dictionary or even a religious book, all by changing the book cover or colours. For example, a cookbook would look great in red, a graduation book looks good in brown, and religious books look great in white or black, but you can't go wrong whatever colour you choose. You can add a book title simply by using your alphabet cutters. Virtually all of the figurines would look great with this cake, but it could also stand alone as a cake in its own right.

MATERIALS

600 g (1 lb 5 oz) coloured icing (display board)
20 cm (8 in) square cake
1.2 kg (2 lb 10 oz) ganache
100 ml (3½ fl oz) syrup
Cornflour (cornstarch) in a shaker
1.5 kg (3 lb 5 oz) white icing (cake)
600 g (1 lb 5 oz) purple icing (book cover)
100 g (3½ oz) purple icing (border)
50 g (1¾ oz) yellow icing (bookmark)
100 g (3½ oz) orange icing (message)

EQUIPMENT

Ganaching tools
Plastic/metal scraper
Cranked palette knife
Serrated knife
20 cm (8 in) square board (set-up)
35 cm (14 in) square board (display)
Large and small rolling pins
Smoother
Small sharp kitchen knife
Small sheet of vinyl or plastic
Flexi-scraper
Pastry brush
Medium paintbrush
Ruler or comb scraper
Alphabet cutters (optional)
Pasta machine (optional, for rolling icing)

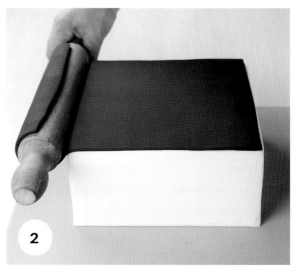

COVER THE DISPLAY BOARD

Knead the coloured icing to a pliable consistency, then roll out to 3 mm (⅛ in) thick. Cover the display board as per instructions on page 181.

GANACHE THE CAKE

Follow the general instructions on how to ganache a square cake on page 31.

COVER THE CAKE AND MAKE PAGES

Knead the white icing to a pliable consistency, then roll out to 3 mm (⅛ in) thick. Follow the instructions on how to cover a square cake on page 35.

While the icing is still soft, indent three adjoining outside edges with a ruler or comb scraper to create the impression of book pages (photo 1).

Allow the icing to dry, then place your cake on your display board.

MAKE THE BOOK COVER

Using your ruler, measure the area where you will need to place the icing for the front cover of the book, as well as the spine. Once you have the measurements, add 1 cm (½ in).

Knead the 600 g (1 lb 5 oz) purple icing to a pliable consistency, then roll out to 3 mm (⅛ in) thick. Cut the icing you require according to your measurements.

Use the same techniques to cover as you would for a whole cake. Cover the top of the cake (front cover of the book) first, then roll the icing around to cover the spine (photo 2). If you need to trim the icing, do so with a knife.

Once the icing is in its perfect position, lift the purple icing cover and brush with water underneath to secure it in place (photo 3).

When you cover the top of the book, make sure you have a little bit of overhang to give the appearance of a proper book front cover — 5 mm (¼ in) will be sufficient. Manipulate this into place.

3

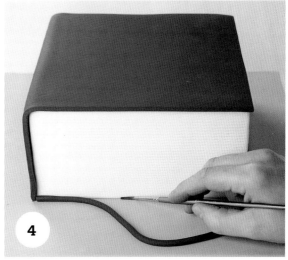

4

BORDER

Measure three sides of your cake — it should be about 60 cm (24 in) in total. This is the length of the icing roll you will need to form your border.

Knead the 100 g (3½ oz) purple icing to a pliable consistency. With the help of your icing smoother, roll the icing into a thin sausage (see page 183).

Brush a line of water on the base of the cake. Carefully place the thin icing roll around the bottom, to form a border or book cover trim (photo 4). Carefully smooth the joining lines.

BOOKMARK

Knead the yellow icing to a pliable consistency, then roll it out to 2 mm (¹⁄₁₆ in) thick. Cut a strip about 10 cm (4 in) long and 2–3 cm (¾–1¼ in) wide. Cut a 'V' out of one end of the bookmark, or make small cuts along one end to give it a frayed effect.

Cover with a sheet of vinyl or plastic to stop it drying out.

To give the illusion that the bookmark is coming out of the cake, poke a knife into the cake and make a slit big enough to hold your bookmark.

Brush a line of water from the cut you have made, down to the end of the book, onto the board.

Place the bookmark into the book by delicately using your knife to edge it in. Place the bookmark along the water mark to secure it to the board.

WRITE YOUR MESSAGE

Knead the orange icing to a pliable consistency, then roll out to 1 mm (¹⁄₃₂ in) thick. Using alphabet cutters, cut out your message.

Brush the back of the letters with a little water and stick them on the cake board.

BEACH CAKE

This cake is fantastic if you are new to decorating; there is loads of room for error as the form is free-flowing and organic. Making a dome cake is relatively easy, but looks very impressive, and creating sand from icing is a lot of fun. If you want to get creative you can add surfboards, seaweed, beach towels and flags. These additional decorations are not at all difficult — you just need some icing and a bit of imagination. Many figurine characters in this book would love to hang out on the beach: especially the Hip hop dudes and Snow-surfing penguins.

MATERIALS

600 g (1 lb 5 oz) blue icing (display board)
22 cm (9 in) round cake
1.2 kg (2 lb 10 oz) ganache
100 ml (3½ fl oz) syrup
Cornflour (cornstarch) in shaker
1.2 kg (2 lb 10 oz) white icing (cake)
200 g (7 oz) raw sugar (sand)
400 g (14 oz) royal icing (sand)
Caramel brown food colour (sand)
500 g (1 lb 2 oz) royal icing (waves)
Royal blue icing paste (waves)
Teal icing paste (waves)
100 g (3½ oz) optional-coloured icing
  (message)

EQUIPMENT

Ganaching tools
Plastic/metal scraper
Cranked palette knife
Serrated knife
25 cm (10 in) round board (set-up)
35 cm (14 in) round board (display)
Large and small rolling pins
Smoother
Small sharp kitchen knife
Flexi-scraper
Pastry brush
Medium paintbrush
Alphabet cutters (optional)

COVER THE DISPLAY BOARD

Knead the blue icing to a pliable consistency, then roll out to 3 mm (⅛ in) thick. Cover the display board as per instructions on page 181.

SHAPE AND GANACHE THE CAKE

Follow the general instructions on how to prepare and ganache a dome cake on pages 39–40.

COVER THE CAKE

Knead the white icing to a pliable consistency, then roll out to 3 mm (⅛ in) thick. Follow the instructions on how to cover a dome cake on pages 40–41.

Allow the icing to dry, then place your cake on your display board.

MAKE THE SAND

Mix the raw sugar and 400 g (14 oz) royal icing together. Add one drop of caramel brown food colour at a time until you get a sand colour (photo 1).

Working quickly, use your palette knife to cover the dome with the sand icing, using your palette knife to rough up the surface. Try to avoid getting your icing on the board.

MAKE WAVES

Take your 500 g (1 lb 2 oz) royal icing and fold in the royal blue and teal colours. To create a two-tone effect, try not to mix the colours together completely.

Use a palette knife to create waves at the base of your cake; start at the bottom of the cake and flick the waves out (photo 2).

WRITE YOUR MESSAGE

Knead the optional-coloured icing to a pliable consistency, then roll out to 1 mm (1/32 in) thick.

Using alphabet cutters, cut out your message (photo 3). Brush the back of the letters with a little water and stick them on the cake board.

BIG STAGE

This design is so versatile and works with nearly all the figurine characters: after all, everyone wants to be in front of an audience! Some features that will impress your guests are the wooden boards and curtains, both of which are relatively easy to make. Traditional colours such as red look fantastic, but please remember that red icing is more difficult to work with (see instructions on page 179). Royal blue or purple also look great, and are a little easier to handle than red. My imagination goes into overdrive with this design — all of a sudden I am seeing the characters in this book transform into magicians … and the perfect message would of course have to be: ABRACADABRAH!

MATERIALS

600 g (1 lb 5 oz) white icing (display board)
20 cm (8 in) square cake
1.2 kg (2 lb 10 oz) ganache
100 ml (3½ fl oz) syrup
Cornflour (cornstarch) in shaker
1.5 kg (3 lb 5 oz) pale green icing (cake)
Brown food colour
Decorating alcohol
Edible silver dust (optional)
300 g (10½ oz) dark green icing (curtains)
100 g (3½ oz) red icing (message)

EQUIPMENT

Ganaching tools
Plastic/metal scraper
Cranked palette knife
Serrated knife
10 x 20 cm (4 x 8 in) rectangle board (set-up)
35 cm (14 in) square board (display)
Large and small rolling pins
Smoother
Small sharp kitchen knife
Frilling tool
Flexi-scraper
Pastry brush
Medium paintbrush
Ruler
Wooden skewers
Pasta machine (optional)

COVER THE DISPLAY BOARD

Knead the white icing to a pliable consistency, then roll out to 3 mm (⅛ in) thick. Cover the display board as per instructions on page 181.

SHAPE AND GANACHE THE WALL

Follow the general instructions on how to prepare and ganache a wall cake on page 36.

COVER THE CAKE

Knead the pale green icing to a pliable consistency, then roll out to 3 mm (⅛ in) thick. Follow the instructions on how to cover a wall cake on pages 37–38.

Allow the icing to dry.

MAKE FLOORBOARDS

While the icing on the display board is still soft, score it with the back of a knife, using a ruler to space the floorboard design (photo 1).

For added effect, use your frilling tool or a small nozzle to indent tiny holes for the 'nails' in the floorboards.

Mix your brown food colour with a little decorating alcohol and test the colour on a piece of scrap icing first. Paint your floorboards using a pastry brush (photo 2). Allow to dry for an hour or so.

Transfer your cake from the set-up board to the floorboards, setting the cake on the back third of the board to leave room for the figurines.

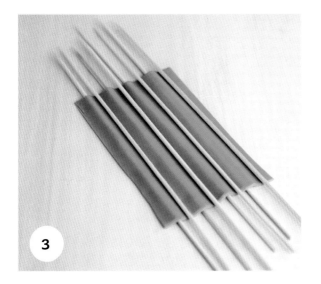

3

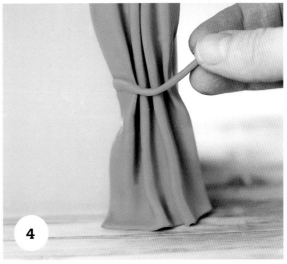

4

Optional: For extra detail after the floorboards are dry, mix edible silver dust with decorating alcohol, and with a fine paintbrush paint the nails in silver.

MAKE THE CURTAINS

Knead the dark green icing to a pliable consistency, then roll out to 1 mm (¹/₃₂ in) thick. Cut out the following pieces from the icing:

   For the sides: two 12 x 14 cm (4½ x 6 in) rectangles

   For the front top: one 10 x 15 cm (4 x 6 in) rectangle

   For the back: one 10 x 24 cm (4 x 9½ in) rectangle

   For over the front edge: two 10 x 18 cm (4 x 7 in) rectangles.

Thread your wooden skewers alternately over and under each piece of icing (photo 3). Now remove the skewers from the icing.

Immediately attach the curtains to the cake — if the icing is still soft, it can be manipulated to fit more easily. First attach your hanging side curtains to the cake, then follow with the box drapes.

Gather the 'curtain' at the top, then place it on your cake with a small amount of water.

Take small pieces of the dark green icing and roll them into balls. Roll the balls into thin sausages, then stick them onto your curtains with a dab of water to form the curtain tie-backs (photo 4).

WRITE YOUR MESSAGE

Knead the red icing to a pliable consistency, then roll out to 1 mm (¹/₃₂ in) thick. Using alphabet cutters, cut out your message.

Brush the back of the letters with a little water and stick them on the cake board.

CANDY FLOSS CLOUDS

In terms of cuteness, the sky is the limit with this cake! I was inspired by Japanese Kawaii designs and really wanted to create a cartoon fantasy feel. You can add different elements to the cake such as stars, lollipops, hearts or even raindrops — for inspiration, search for Kawaii on the internet. Using the simple template technique on page 183, you can then incorporate so many additional elements. When I designed this cake I did have girls in mind, but it would also be perfect for younger children and even christenings.

MATERIALS

600 g (1 lb 5 oz) blue icing (display board)

20 cm (8 in) square cake

1.2 kg (2 lb 10 oz) ganache

100 ml (3½ fl oz) syrup

Cornflour (cornstarch) in shaker

1.5 kg (3 lb 5 oz) blue icing (cake)

20 g (¾ oz) red icing (rainbow)

20 g (¾ oz) orange icing (rainbow)

20 g (¾ oz) yellow icing (rainbow)

20 g (¾ oz) green icing (rainbow)

20 g (¾ oz) blue icing (rainbow)

20 g (¾ oz) purple icing (rainbow)

100 g (3½ oz) white icing (clouds)

EQUIPMENT

Ganaching tools

Plastic/metal scraper

Cranked palette knife

Serrated knife

10 x 20 cm (4 x 8 in) rectangle board (set-up)

35 cm (14 in) round board (display)

Large and small rolling pins

Smoother

Small sharp kitchen knife

Flexi-scraper

Pastry brush

Medium paintbrush

Baking paper

2B pencil

Scissors

Zip-lock bag

Pin (optional)

Pasta machine (optional, for rolling icing)

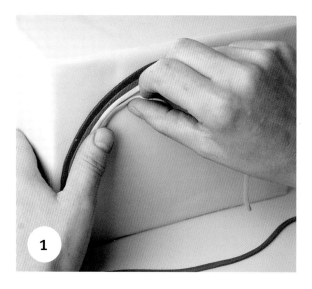

1

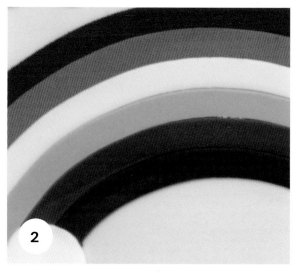

2

COVER THE DISPLAY BOARD

Knead the 600 g (1 lb 5 oz) blue icing to a pliable consistency, then roll out to 3 mm (⅛ in) thick. Cover the display board as per instructions on page 181.

SHAPE AND GANACHE THE WALL

Follow the general instructions on how to prepare and ganache a wall cake on page 36.

COVER THE CAKE

Knead the 1.5 kg (3 lb 5 oz) blue icing to a pliable consistency, then roll out to 3 mm (⅛ in) thick.

Follow the instructions on how to cover a wall cake on pages 37–38.

Allow the icing to dry, then place your cake on your display board.

MAKE TEMPLATES

Using a photocopier, enlarge the rainbow and cloud templates opposite. Trace the templates onto a sheet of baking paper with a 2B pencil and cut around them.

MAKE A RAINBOW

Transfer the rainbow template design to the front of your cake (see page 183).

Mix all of your rainbow colour icings and roll them into smooth, crack-free balls. Place them in a zip-lock bag so they don't dry out.

Option 1

Roll out the coloured icings to 2 mm (¹⁄₁₆ in) thick. Using your baking paper template as a guide, cut the rainbow arc shapes using a small sharp knife.

Brush the back of the rainbow arcs with a little water and stick them to the front of your cake.

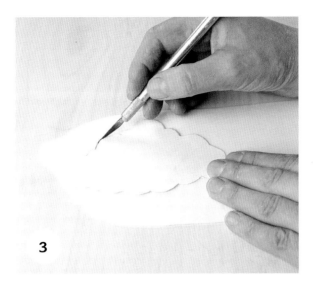

3

Option 2

Roll out the coloured icings to 2 mm (¹⁄₁₆ in) thick. Roll them, separately, through a pasta machine on the fettuccine setting, for the rainbow arc shapes.

Stick them to the front of your cake with a dab of water (photo 1).

Option 3

Roll out the coloured icings into evenly sized thin sausages (see page 183), then flatten them.

Stick them onto the front of your cake with a dab of water to form a rainbow arc (photo 2).

ROLL OUT THE CLOUDS

Knead the 100 g (3½ oz) white icing to a pliable consistency, then roll out to 1 mm (¹⁄₃₂ in) thick.

Place the cloud template on top of the icing and cut out cloud shapes (photo 3).

Stick the clouds on the cake and the board with a dab of water.

TEMPLATES — AT 50%

CARTOON CAKE

If you love cartoons, then you know that this is how a birthday cake is supposed to look! I love this design for its luxurious icing and vibrant colours — it's a cake design that is perfect for everyone, not just kids. Some great colour combinations include a white base with gelato colours such as raspberry and mocha, or mix it up with sorbet colours such as lemon and pistachio. If you are placing characters on the board, make sure you set the cake back to accommodate them. Characters that look great with this cake include the Softie bears, Pig & Pepper and Sporty dogs.

MATERIALS

600 g (1 lb 5 oz) white icing (display board)
22 cm (9 in) round cake
1.2 kg (2 lb 10 oz) ganache
100 ml (3½ fl oz) syrup
Cornflour (cornstarch) in shaker
1.5 kg (3 lb 5 oz) brown icing (cake)
400 g (14 oz) pink icing (cake icing top)
100 g (3½ oz) pink icing (middle icing strip)
12 x 10 g (¼ oz) balls of red icing (cherries)
Green florist's tape
Glaze
100 g (3½ oz) white royal icing
100 g (3½ oz) optional-coloured icing
   (message)

EQUIPMENT

Ganaching tools
Plastic/metal scraper
Cranked palette knife
Serrated knife
22 cm (9 in) round board (set-up)
35 cm (14 in) round board (display)
Large and small rolling pins
Smoother
Small sharp kitchen knife
Flexi-scraper
Pastry brush
Medium paintbrush
Alphabet cutters (optional)
Pasta machine (optional, for rolling icing)
Frilling tool
1 cm (½ in) star nozzle
Piping bag
Pizza wheel

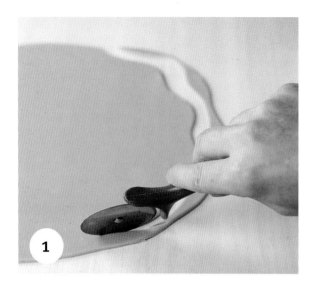

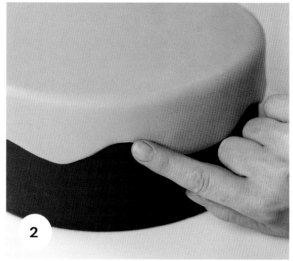

COVER THE DISPLAY BOARD

Knead the white icing to a pliable consistency, then roll out to 3 mm (⅛ in) thick. Cover the display board as per instructions on page 181.

GANACHE THE CAKE

Follow the general instructions on how to ganache a round cake on pages 28–30.

COVER THE CAKE

Knead the brown icing to a pliable consistency, then roll out to 3 mm (⅛ in) thick. Follow the instructions on how to cover a round cake on pages 32–34. Allow the icing to dry.

Place your cake on your display board, setting it back to make room at the front for your figurines (don't set the cake dead-centre on the board).

MAKE THE PINK TOP ICING

Measure the top section of the cake to be covered with pink icing and increase this by 10 cm (4 in). Brush the area with a small amount of water.

Knead the 400 g (14 oz) pink icing to a pliable consistency, then roll out to 3 mm (⅛ in) thick.

Using a pizza wheel, cut a wave pattern around the edge of the icing circle, to form the 'drips' (photo 1). You can do this freehand, or if you prefer, make your own template for this.

Place the icing on top of the cake, then smooth and round the drip edges with your fingers (photo 2).

Smooth the top and the edge of the cake with your flexi-scraper.

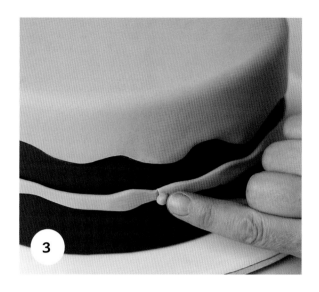

MAKE THE PINK MIDDLE ICING STRIP

Measure the circumference of the cake. Knead the 100 g (3½ oz) pink icing to a pliable consistency. With the help of your icing smoother, roll it into an uneven sausage.

Brush a line of water around the middle of the cake, then carefully roll the cord around it, starting at the back.

Use a small ball of icing to cover the joining line (photo 3), then flatten the icing softly against the cake.

MAKE THE CHERRIES

Roll the eight balls of red icing into smooth balls, tapering them lightly on one side to create the base of the cherry.

With your frilling tool, make an indent in the top of each. Into each one, insert a stem, made from a short length of twisted green florist's tape, slightly bent (photo 4). Brush the cherries with glaze.

PIPE THE CREAM

Using a piping bag fitted with a 1 cm (½ in) star nozzle, pipe 12 rosettes of white royal icing around the top edge of the cake. It's a really good idea to first practise your piping on a piece of baking paper before attempting to pipe on the cake.

Place a cherry on each rosette before the icing sets.

WRITE YOUR MESSAGE

Knead your optional-coloured icing to a pliable consistency, then roll out to 1 mm (¹/₃₂ in) thick.

Using alphabet cutters, cut out your message. Brush the back of the letters with a little water and stick them on the cake board.

COOKING POT

This cake looks amazing — imagine receiving it for a birthday! Although it looks complex, it is fairly easy to create. Don't let the lid put you off: it is actually part of the cake icing, just decorated to look like a separate lid. This cooking pot is actually identical to one my mother used in the 1970s! The cooking pot shown here is lime green, but you can make it any colour you like. The best colours are bright ones such as orange, red, green and teal. Apart from the Fat rats, all of the characters like to cook … the Little nipper lifesaver lobsters are perfect!

WHAT YOU NEED

MATERIALS

600 g (1 lb 5 oz) grey icing (display board)

22 cm (9 in) round cake

1.2 kg (2 lb 10 oz) ganache

100 ml (3½ fl oz) syrup

Cornflour (cornstarch) in shaker

1.5 kg (3 lb 5 oz) lime green icing (cake)

30 g (1 oz) black icing (lid handle)

100 g (3½ oz) lime green icing (pot handles)

80 g (2¾ oz) red icing (flame)

80 g (2¾ oz) yellow icing (flame)

80 g (2¾ oz) orange icing (flame)

100 g (3½ oz) optional-coloured icing
   (message)

EQUIPMENT

Ganaching tools

Plastic/metal scraper

Cranked palette knife

Serrated knife

2 x 22 cm (9 in) round boards (set-up + 1)

35 cm (14 in) round board (display)

Large and small rolling pins

Smoother

Small sharp kitchen knife

Flexi-scraper

Pastry brush

Frilling tool

Circle cutters

Medium paintbrush

Stitching tool (optional)

Pizza wheel (optional)

Alphabet cutters (optional)

Pasta machine (optional, for rolling icing)

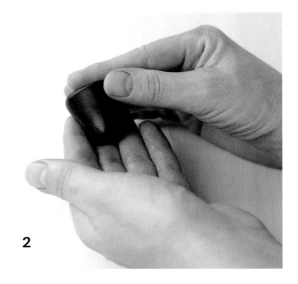

COVER THE DISPLAY BOARD

Knead the grey icing to a pliable consistency, then roll out to 3 mm (⅛ in) thick. Cover the display board as per instructions on page 181.

GANACHE THE CAKE

Follow the general instructions on how to ganache a round cake on pages 28–30.

COVER THE CAKE

Knead the 1.5 kg (3 lb 5 oz) lime green icing to a pliable consistency, then roll out to 3 mm (⅛ in) thick.

Follow the instructions on how to cover a round cake on pages 32–34.

While the icing is still soft, mark the lid (see next step).

MARK THE LID

Place a 22 cm (9 in) round board on top of the cake. Score the icing around the edge of the board with a frilling tool (photo 1), to mark the outer edge of the lid.

For a realistic lid, repeat the process with an 18 cm (7 in), 13 cm (5 in) and 7.5 cm (3 in) board and template. This will give the illusion of a slightly dome-shaped lid.

Place your cake on your display board, setting it back to make room at the front for your figurines (don't set the cake dead-centre on the board).

MAKE THE LID HANDLE

Roll your black icing into a smooth ball. Shape it into a handle with your fingers (photo 2).

If you like, use the back of a knife to make a criss-cross pattern on top of the handle.

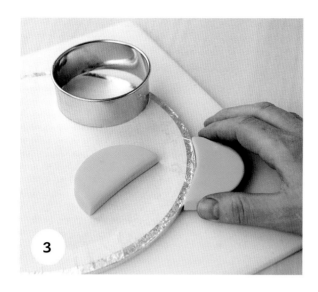

MAKE THE POT HANDLES

Roll your 100 g (3½ oz) ball of lime green icing out to 1 cm (½ in) thick.

Using an 8 cm (3¼ in) circle cutter, cut out a circle. Cut the circle in half; these two halves will be your handles.

Place the handles on the side of your board, then manipulate them to fit the curve of the board (photo 3). By using the board to shape your handles, you know that they will fit perfectly to the sides of your cake. Allow the handles to dry.

When the handles have hardened, brush the inside edges with a little water and stick them to the sides of your pot.

MAKE THE FLAMES

Partially mix together the red, yellow and orange icing to give a streaky effect (see marbling techniques, page 180).

Carefully roll the icing out to 2 mm (1/16 in) thick. Using a sharp knife or pizza wheel, cut the icing into triangle shapes of various sizes to replicate flames (photo 4).

Brush the bottom bit of the cake with water and stick on the flames, overlapping them slightly as you go.

WRITE YOUR MESSAGE

Knead your optional-coloured icing to a pliable consistency, then roll out to 1 mm (1/32 in) thick. Using alphabet cutters, cut out your message.

Brush the back of the letters with a little water and stick them on the cake board.

GRAFFITI WALL

This cake is so effective because it is high, and allows you to put whatever message you wish across the front for maximum impact. The design is perfect for all age groups, and the colours can be altered to appeal: for example a brown wall for a more realistic effect, a red wall for children, or just a plain white wall for a cleaner cake. When choosing the message, shorter single words work best, as you can use a larger font size. The best thing about this cake is how well it photographs, because it is high, and because it uses the board so well to create a 'scene'. It also works so well with virtually all of the figurine characters in this book, from Superheroes to Sporty dogs and everything in between.

MATERIALS

600 g (1 lb 5 oz) green icing (display board)

20 cm (8 in) square cake

1.2 kg (2 lb 10 oz) ganache

100 ml (3½ fl oz) syrup

Cornflour (cornstarch) in shaker

1.5 kg (3 lb 5 oz) brown icing (cake)

100 g (3½ oz) optional-coloured icing
   (graffiti)

EQUIPMENT

Ganaching tools

Plastic/metal scraper

Cranked palette knife

Serrated knife

10 x 20 cm (4 x 8 in) rectangle board (set-up)

35 cm (14 in) round board (display)

Large and small rolling pins

Smoother

Small sharp kitchen knife

Flexi-scraper

Pastry brush

Medium paintbrush

Ruler

Baking paper

2B pencil

Scissors

Pin (optional)

Pasta machine (optional)

Alphabet cutters (optional)

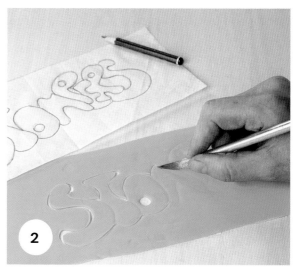

COVER THE DISPLAY BOARD

Knead the green icing to a pliable consistency, then roll out to 3 mm (⅛ in) thick. Cover the display board as per instructions on page 181.

SHAPE AND GANACHE THE WALL

Follow the general instructions on how to prepare and ganache a wall cake on page 36.

COVER THE CAKE

Knead the brown icing to a pliable consistency, then roll out to 3 mm (⅛ in) thick. Follow the instructions on how to cover a wall cake on pages 37–38.

While the icing is still soft, use a ruler to indent the pattern of bricks on the wall (photo 1).

Allow the icing to dry for an hour or so, then place your cake on the display board.

MAKE THE GRAFFITI TEMPLATES

Using a photocopier, enlarge the stomper graffiti template opposite. Trace the template onto a sheet of baking paper with a 2B pencil.

Alternatively, make your own template — perhaps with the birthday person's name. Using your computer, you could find a font you like and create a message to the size you want using the letters you want.

Another option is to simply use alphabet cutters to write the graffiti.

APPLY THE GRAFFITI

Knead the optional-coloured icing to a pliable consistency, then roll out to about 1 mm (¹⁄₃₂ in) thick.

Place your graffiti template on top of the icing and trace over it. This will leave an indent on the icing. Lift the template off, then cut out the graffiti image with a small sharp knife (photo 2).

Brush the back of the letters with a little water and stick them on the wall or the cake board.

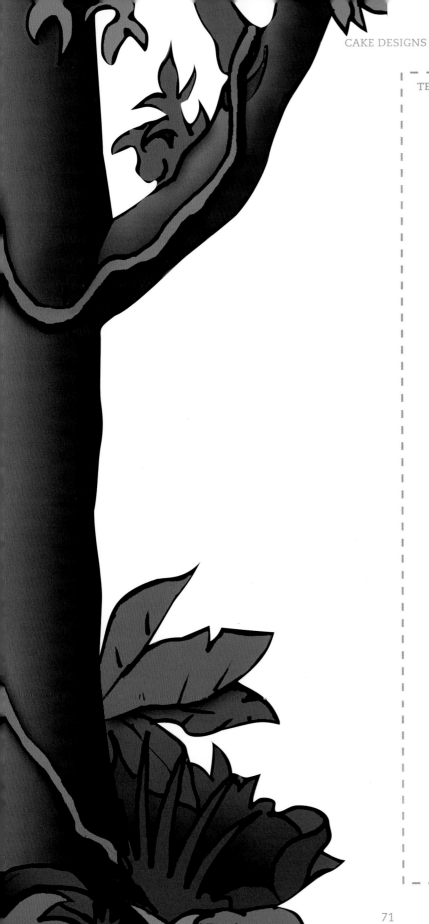

TEMPLATE — AT 50%

GRAVEYARD

Of all the cakes, this is the grossest and the easiest. There is no fondant covering it — the 'dirt' on top is actually cake crumbs. The dome shape is easy to create, and the shape is free and easy. Although, as a spooky graveyard, it's a terrifying sight, it works well for figurine characters who would also be found on the ground, such as the Ninja rabbits accompanied by a few carrots, the Sporty dogs or even a Baby dragon. There is lots of versatility with this cake, and it really is very yummy! If you wish to have a brown cake, you will need to use chocolate cake; white cakes with white chocolate ganache could be a great alternative. If you are making Mrs Zucker's bits & pieces, the red velvet cake (page 25) would be a fabulous choice.

WHAT YOU NEED

MATERIALS

600 g (1 lb 5 oz) dark green icing
  (display board)
22 cm (9 in) round cake
1.5 kg (3 lb 5 oz) ganache
100 ml (3½ fl oz) syrup
Cornflour (cornstarch) in shaker
200 g (7 oz) chocolate ganache (intestines)
3 tablespoons piping gel
100 g (3½ oz) red royal icing
200 g (7 oz) optional-coloured icing
  (message)

EQUIPMENT

Ganaching tools
Plastic/metal scraper
Cranked palette knife
Serrated knife
25 cm (10 in) round board (set-up)
35 cm (14 in) round board (display)
Large and small rolling pins
Smoother
Small sharp kitchen knife
Flexi-scraper
Pastry brush
Medium paintbrush
Baking paper
Piping bag
1 cm (½ in) plain nozzle
Alphabet cutters

COVER THE DISPLAY BOARD

Knead the dark green icing to a pliable consistency, then roll out to 3 mm (⅛ in) thick. Cover the display board as per instructions on page 181.

SHAPE AND GANACHE THE CAKE

Follow the general instructions on how to prepare and ganache a dome cake on pages 39–40. However, instead of using all of the cake shavings to build your dome, reserve about 1½ cups and crumble it in a thin layer onto a plate.

Allow to stand at room temperature for 1–2 hours to dry out the crumbs. (This will be to cover your cake, to create the 'soil'.)

Allow the cake to dry, then place your cake on your display board.

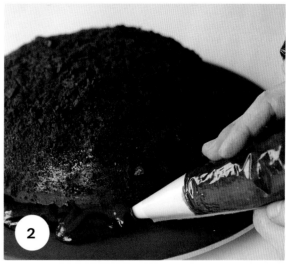

SPRINKLE THE CAKE WITH CRUMBS

Cover the exposed bits of board with baking paper to avoid it being marked.

Instead of covering your cake with fondant icing, crumble your dry cake crumbs over the cake to replicate soil (photo 1). The top will be the most important, as this is where the figurines are usually placed.

MAKE THE INTESTINE BORDER

Mix the chocolate ganache with the royal icing and the piping gel — but don't completely blend it, as we're after a streaky effect.

Using a piping bag fitted with a 1 cm (½ in) plain nozzle, pipe the ganache mixture to make a border around the base of your cake (photo 2). There are no real rules as to how your border should look.

WRITE YOUR MESSAGE

Knead your optional-coloured icing to a pliable consistency, then roll out to 1 mm (¹/₃₂ in) thick. Using alphabet cutters, cut out your message.

Brush the back of the letters with a little water and stick them on the cake board.

MAN IN THE MOON

This is one of the easier designs in this book, and one of the most effective. Moon cakes lend themselves to fantasy or space themes, but the characters that would make the most of this cake would definitely be the Superheroes. Have fun with the colours: a red moon could make a great 'Mars' cake for crazy characters like the Video nuts or Hip hop dudes. A realistic grey moon would be great for spacemen Stompers; you could even colour your Stompers white so it looks like they are wearing space suits. If you want to simplify the decoration, the face and nose are optional.

MATERIALS

600 g (1 lb 5 oz) black icing (display board)
22 cm (9 in) round cake
1.2 kg (2 lb 10 oz) ganache
100 ml (3½ fl oz) syrup
Cornflour (cornstarch) in shaker
20 g (¾ oz) yellow icing (nose)
1.5 kg (3 lb 5 oz) yellow icing (cake)
10 g (¼ oz) white icing (eyes)
5 g (⅛ oz) black icing (eyes)
20 g (¾ oz) red icing (mouth)
200 g (7 oz) optional-coloured icing
   (message)

EQUIPMENT

Ganaching tools
Plastic/metal scraper
Cranked palette knife
Serrated knife
25 cm (10 in) round board (set-up)
35 cm (14 in) round board (display)
Large and small rolling pins
Smoother
Small sharp kitchen knife
Balling tool
Flexi-scraper
Baking paper
Pastry brush
Medium paintbrush
Alphabet cutters
Frilling tool
2B pencil
Scissors

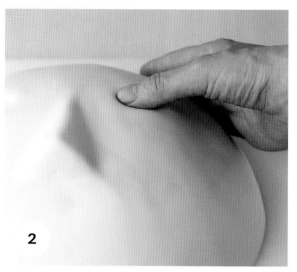

COVER THE DISPLAY BOARD

Knead the black icing to a pliable consistency, then roll out to 3 mm (⅛ in) thick. Cover the display board as per instructions on page 181.

SHAPE AND GANACHE THE CAKE

Follow the general instructions on how to prepare and ganache a dome cake on pages 39–40.

SHAPE THE NOSE

Roll your 20 g (¾ oz) piece of yellow icing into a smooth, crack-free ball. Mould a nose from the ball — there are no hard-and-fast rules on how to do this; your nose can be any shape and size you wish.

Stick the nose onto the ganached cake with a dab of water (photo 1), smoothing the join marks between the nose and the moon with your finger. You need to do this step before covering the cake with fondant.

COVER THE CAKE

Knead your 1.5 kg (3 lb 5 oz) of yellow icing to a pliable consistency, then roll out to 3 mm (⅛ in) thick.

Follow the instructions on how to cover a dome cake on pages 40–41. When you smooth the icing over the dome, smooth the cake with your flexi-scraper.

MAKE THE EYES

Using your thumb or the back of a balling tool, indent two eye sockets on the moon (photo 2).

Roll your white icing into two small balls, then flatten them between your fingers. Brush the back with a dab of water and place the white eyes in the indents.

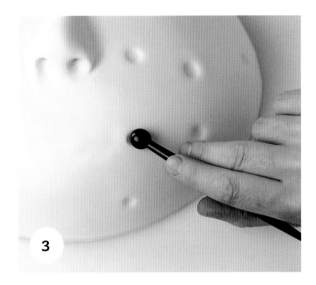

3

4

Roll two smaller balls of black icing, then place them on top of the eyes with a dab of water to form the pupils.

MARK THE NOSTRILS
Using a frilling tool, indent two holes for the nostrils.

MARK THE CRATERS
Using the balling tool, indent shallow hollows all over the moon to replicate the moon's surface (photo 3).

MAKE THE MOUTH
Draw up a simple template of a mouth shape. Roll out your ball of red icing to 2 mm ($1/16$ in) thick. Using a 2B pencil, trace your mouth template onto a sheet of baking paper.

Cut out your mouth shape and place it on top of the red icing. Using a small sharp knife, cut out the mouth shape from the icing (see photo 3, page 59).

Using the back of a knife, indent a line across the middle of the mouth, to create the join mark of the top and bottom lip (photo 4).

Stick the mouth onto the moon with a thin line of water.

WRITE YOUR MESSAGE
Knead your optional-coloured icing to a pliable consistency, then roll out to 1 mm ($1/32$ in) thick. Using alphabet cutters, cut out your message.

Brush the back of the letters with a little water and stick them on the cake board.

MARTIAL ARTS RING

This cake is very simple, and all the colours can be adjusted. I recommend changing the colour of the martial arts belt to match the skill level of the recipient; however, a black belt will provide some great inspiration! Thinking a little left field, this cake could also become a picnic scene … the Softie bears would love to catch up here for sandwiches and tea. Just trim the belt tails flush to the bottom of the cake — you can even change the base cake colour to green, and the board too if you wish, and hey presto: a grassy knoll with a picnic rug. If you have any difficulty with tears in your icing, please remember you can cover these with stars or other cut-out decorations.

MATERIALS

600 g (1 lb 5 oz) blue icing (display board)
22 cm (9 in) round cake
1.2 kg (2 lb 10 oz) ganache
100 ml (3½ fl oz) syrup
Cornflour (cornstarch) in shaker
1.5 kg (3 lb 5 oz) white icing (cake)
150 g (5½ oz) black icing (belt)
150 g (5½ oz) red icing (mat)
100 g (3½ oz) optional-coloured icing
   (message)

EQUIPMENT

Ganaching tools
Plastic/metal scraper
Cranked palette knife
Serrated knife
22 cm (9 in) round board (set-up)
35 cm (14 in) round board (display)
Large and small rolling pins
Smoother
Small sharp kitchen knife
Flexi-scraper
Pastry brush
Medium paintbrush
Tape measure
Ruler
Stitching tool
Small sheet of vinyl or plastic
Alphabet cutters (optional)
Pasta machine (optional, for rolling icing)

COVER THE DISPLAY BOARD

Knead the blue icing to a pliable consistency, then roll out to 3 mm (⅛ in) thick. Cover the display board as per instructions on page 181.

GANACHE THE CAKE

Follow the general instructions on how to prepare and ganache a round cake on pages 28–30.

COVER THE CAKE

Knead the white icing to a pliable consistency, then roll out to 3 mm (⅛ in) thick. Follow the instructions on how to cover a round cake on pages 32–34.

Allow the icing to dry, then place your cake on your display board.

MAKE THE BELT

Knead the black icing to a pliable consistency, then use one of the following two methods to create the belt.

Option 1

Measure the circumference of your cake using a tape measure. Now add an extra 5 cm (2 in) to the length.

Using a rolling pin, roll your icing out a bit longer than this length, in a rough rectangle shape.

Using a ruler, cut your icing to the length you had measured, in a long strip that is about 2.5 cm (1 in) wide.

Using your stitching tool, imprint each long side of the strip to replicate the stitching on a real martial arts belt (photo 1).

Brush a line of water around the base of the cake. Carefully wrap the belt around the base of the cake, making sure the strip joins at the front.

Option 2

Measure the circumference of your cake using a tape measure. Now add an extra 5 cm (2 in) to the length, and make the width about 2.5cm (1 in) wider than a ruler's width.

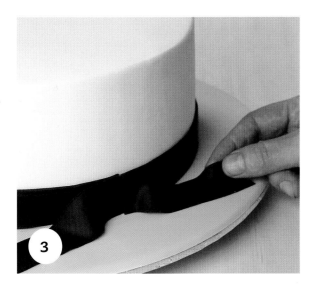

Brush a line of water around the base of the cake and carefully wrap the belt around the base of the cake, ensuring the join is at the front.

Now take a ruler and use it as a guide to neatly cut along the top edge with a clean sharp knife (photo 2).

MAKE THE KNOT

Cut two strips of black icing, each about 2.5 x 10 cm (1 x 4 in). Cut a third strip measuring 2.5 x 2.5 cm (1 x 1 in).

Using your stitching tool, imprint the sides of each strip with a pattern to replicate a real martial arts belt. Cover them with vinyl or plastic so they don't dry out.

Place the two longer strips of icing across the join and onto the cake board with a line of water (photo 3).

Use the smallest piece of icing to replicate a knot. Place it over the join where all the strips meet with a thin line of water (photo 4).

ROLL OUT THE MAT

Knead the red icing into a pliable consistency, then roll out to about 2 mm ($\frac{1}{16}$ in) thick.

Cut an 18 cm (7 in) square from the icing, then place it on top of your cake with a small amount of water.

WRITE YOUR MESSAGE

Knead your optional-coloured icing to a pliable consistency, then roll out to 1 mm ($\frac{1}{32}$ in) thick. Using alphabet cutters, cut out your message.

Brush the back of the letters with a little water and stick them on the cake board.

VIDEO GAME

This cake is great for anyone who loves video games, especially when topped with the crazy Video nuts. Most computer graphics use a kaleidoscope of amazing colours, so I would encourage you to use these on the cake. Lime greens, blues and reds all look fantastic — but do check our tips on pages 178–179 for using red and black icing, if these colours are your first choice. You can add some extra details to the cake by studying the computer games the cake recipient likes to play. Or you could go one step further by adding a score board message — for example, if the recipient is turning seven, you could write LEVEL 7 on the board using your alphabet cutters! A square cake is a little more challenging than a round cake or a dome, so if this is your first cake you might want to transfer the design to a round cake. Decorating it is very simple and straightforward, though. All you need are great colours and some funky figurines.

MATERIALS

600 g (1 lb 5 oz) blue or purple icing
    (display board)
20 cm (8 in) square cake
1.2 kg (2 lb 10 oz) ganache
100 ml (3½ fl oz) syrup
Cornflour (cornstarch) in shaker
1.5 kg (3 lb 5 oz) black icing (cake)
100 g (3½ oz) blue or purple icing (border)
100 g (3½ oz) blue or purple icing (maze)
200 g (7 oz) white icing (maze balls)
100 g (3½ oz) optional-coloured icing
    (message)

EQUIPMENT

Ganaching tools
Plastic/metal scraper
Cranked palette knife
Serrated knife
20 cm (8 in) square board (set-up)
35 cm (14 in) square board (display)
Large and small rolling pins
Smoother
Small sharp kitchen knife
Flexi-scraper
Pastry brush
Medium paintbrush
Clay gun (optional)
Alphabet cutters

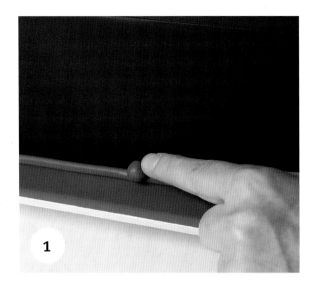

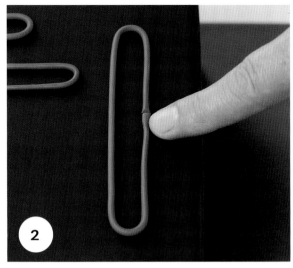

COVER THE DISPLAY BOARD

Knead your 600 g (1 lb 5 oz) blue or purple icing to a pliable consistency, then roll out to 3 mm (⅛ in) thick. Cover the display board as per instructions on page 181.

GANACHE THE CAKE

Follow the general instructions on how to ganache a square cake on page 31.

COVER THE CAKE

Knead the black icing to a pliable consistency, then roll out to 3 mm (⅛ in) thick. Follow the instructions on how to cover a square cake on page 35.

MAKE A BORDER

Knead 100 g (3½ oz) of the blue or purple icing to a pliable consistency. With the help of your icing smoother, roll the icing into a long, thin sausage (see page 183), long enough to wrap around the base of the cake.

Brush a line of water around the base of the cake. Starting at the back, carefully place the sausage around the base of the cake.

Use a small ball of icing to cover the joining line (photo 1), then flatten the icing softly against the cake.

MARK THE MAZE

Knead another 100 g (3½ oz) of the blue or purple icing to a pliable consistency. With the help of your icing smoother, roll the icing into thin sausage lengths of different sizes, to create your maze. The maze can be any configuration you wish.

Brush thin lines of water on top of the cake where you wish to place the maze. Carefully place the sausages into position. Cut the joining lines cleanly, and smooth them with your fingers (photo 2).

Note: If you have one, use a clay gun to make the sausages for the maze. It will save you time, and will ensure the icing sausages are consistently thin.

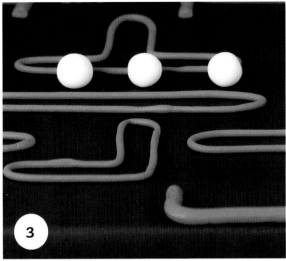

MAKE SOME MAZE BALLS

Knead the white icing to a pliable consistency. With the help of your icing smoother, roll the icing into a sausage.

Using a knife, cut your sausage into small even sections. Roll each section into a ball, then stick them on top of your cake with a dab of water (photo 3).

WRITE YOUR MESSAGE

Knead the optional-coloured icing to a pliable consistency, then roll out to 1 mm (1/32 in) thick.

Using alphabet cutters, cut out your message. Brush the back of the letters with a little water and stick them on the cake board.

SNOW CAP

When I think of heaven, it's always white, soft, fluffy and dreamy, just like this simple cake. This cake uses the Italian buttercream recipe from page 176. You could also use the vanilla buttercream recipe from page 177, but the cake will not be as white.

PREPARE THE CAKE

With your serrated knife, trim the top of the cake to create an even surface. Following the general instructions on page 28, slice the cake into three even layers. Apply buttercream to the bottom and middle layer of the cake, then sandwich the cake together. Place the cake on your display plate or stand. Tuck strips of baking paper underneath the cake to keep your cake neat while you frost it.

CRUMB-COAT THE CAKE

Spread a thin layer of buttercream on the top and sides of the cake to seal in the crumbs (this is called 'crumb-coating'). Chill for 30 minutes, to help stop crumbs working their way into the buttercream.

FROST THE CAKE

Take your palette knife and mound all the remaining buttercream on top of the cake. Start to work the buttercream down the sides of the cake — as rough or smooth as you like. Carefully remove the strips of baking paper before serving the cake.

MATERIALS
22 cm (9 in) round cake
5 cups Italian buttercream

EQUIPMENT
Cranked palette knife
Serrated knife
35 cm (14 in) display plate or
   cake stand
Small sharp kitchen knife
Baking paper

CAKE TOPPERS

HEY KIDS!

Have you ever worked with Play-Doh or Lego? Making a cake topper is very similar, except you make your designs out of sugar!

The sugar you use is called 'fondant icing', and it is the same icing that covers cakes. Fondant icing works exactly like Play-Doh, but you can make it any colour you wish, and it's edible so you can put your creations on the top of a cake.

Here are a few secrets to making the best cake toppers.

STEP 1

Get a fantastic grown-up to help you get all the materials you will need. Let them help you with all the instructions — and maybe even make the cake that your fabulous cake toppers will be placed on.

STEP 2

Be a Cake Designer.

- Think about who the cake is for. The secret to magical cakes is to try to make a unique cake for each person. This means thinking about what people might like. Do they have a special hobby? Or do they have favourite colours?
- Decide which cake toppers you want to make before you start. You can choose the cake toppers you like the best in this book, or even come up with your own designs.
- Once you have decided on your figurines, you can decide what their names are — and whether they are naughty, happy, sleeping, or whatever your characters like to do. You are creating your own little story — this is the most important part of making wonderful cake toppers.
- Speak to a grown-up about the cake design you have chosen to put your toppers on.

STEP 3

Be a Cake Artist.

- With the help of a grown-up, follow the instructions to make your own cake toppers and colour your icing.
- Weigh all the different parts of your figurines and put them to the side. This is important because you don't want to have legs that are too long, or heads that are too small. The quantities need to be spot-on.
- Next you put your cake toppers together, piece by piece. You will have to use some tools including a sharp knife, and of course your fingers!

STEP 4

The final skill you need to make your cake toppers extra special is your **imagination**. Your cake toppers are your creations. You get to decide exactly how they are going to look — it's like a story coming alive.

So let's get started!

NOTES FOR GROWN-UPS

The figurines in this book have been created so that they can be personalised, improved upon or transformed. However, to achieve great results, there are a few hard-and-fast rules, explained below.

When making figurines with children, encourage them to improvise — figurines are a great way to tell a story. Get them to name their figurines, and think about who they're making them for and why. Children relate to feelings, so it's great if they can make a 'happy' or 'naughty' monster, rather than just a 'monster', as this encourages them to use their imagination.

COLOURING THE ICING

See pages 178–179 for tips on colouring fondant icing. Remember that colour pastes are more concentrated and give more intense colours than liquid food colours.

MIXING THE ICING WITH TYLOSE

Once you've coloured your fondant, it's best to mix any larger amounts with Tylose (see Glossary, page 173), to ensure it dries hard.

Tiny amounts of icing, such as those used just for eyes or ears, don't need to be mixed with Tylose. However, do use Tylose for structural elements of the figurines, such as the body, arms and legs (things that can drop off). This is especially essential if the weather is hot and humid.

Make sure you add the Tylose before the icing is measured out. The quantities are not an exact science. For a piece of icing the size of a golf ball, we lightly roll it in Tylose and then mix, remembering you can add but cannot take away. Another formula for larger amounts is 1 teaspoon of Tylose per 450 g (1 lb) of icing.

TIMING

Make your figurines at least a day before you decorate your cake — especially if you are not using Tylose — to allow sufficient drying time. Figurines can in fact be made weeks in advance. However, if you are placing your figurines on a cake iced with buttercream, do so at the last moment.

ALWAYS WORK FROM A BALL

I recommend starting from a ball of fondant icing for all your different icing elements, whatever they may be. A smooth ball, free of cracks, is the best starting point for all the different shapes you need to create. It also ensures that you have kneaded the icing and it is warm, soft and pliable, making it easy to work with.

SUPPORTING THE FIGURINES

Use dried spaghetti to support heads, limbs and standing figurines. If the cake is only for adults, toothpicks are another option.

PLACING THE FIGURINES

You can either place your figurines on your cake with a dab of water, or use dried spaghetti to support them.

STORING FIGURINES

Store your figurines in a cool, dark place — but please don't refrigerate them, as they will 'sweat' and become unmanageable. They need to be kept dry and away from sunlight. Also be careful with humidity.

VIDEO NUTS

In a crazy moment on a rainy day I thought I would get creative and invent my own computer game characters; I call them Video nuts. The best thing about inventing your own characters is that you can give them special talents and abilities that you would love to have yourself. Therefore there are no other gaming heroes I would rather have on my side than these guys.

They are no-holds-barred champions, jumping, flashing, back-flipping, spinning and leaping all over the game, chopping up swathes of enemies like they are dicing onions. They are also monsters and with their claw-like appendages on their fists, they keep cutting through opponents time and again.

The Video nuts are characters in a video game that sees them going through a maze, eating white dots. When they have eaten all the dots on the first level, they are then taken to the next level, which provides new challenges. They stare down their enemies with their crazy eye and munch them down with their fangs, until they win.

If you know someone who loves computer games, these characters are perfect. You can also create your own computer characters, using any colour icing you like. I am sure you have even better ideas than mine! Video games are fantastical and there are no limits, so let your imagination go crazy.

EQUIPMENT
Medium paintbrush
Zip-lock bag
Balling tool
Small kitchen knife
Small rolling pin

MATERIALS – 1 VIDEO NUT
Tylose
10 g (¼ oz) coloured icing (base)
70 g (2½ oz) coloured icing (body)
1 peanut-sized ball of coloured icing (nose)
1 pea-sized ball of coloured icing (hair)
1 pea-sized ball of coloured icing (ear)
1 peanut-sized ball of coloured icing (eyes)
1 pea-sized ball of contrasting coloured icing (eyes)
1 pea-sized ball of black icing (eyes)
1 peanut-sized ball of black icing (mouth)
1 pea-sized ball of red icing (mouth)
1 pea-sized ball of white icing (teeth)

COLOUR THE FONDANT ICING

Mix the colours the day before if possible, to make intense colours easier to work with. For instructions on how to colour fondant icing, see pages 178–179.

MEASURE AND ROLL

Measure each amount of icing required per body part, then roll each into a ball. Place in a zip-lock bag so they don't dry out.

BASE FOR THE BODY

Roll your 10 g (¼ oz) icing into a smooth ball and flatten to about 5 mm (¼ in) thick.

BODY

Make sure your 70 g (2½ oz) ball of icing is smooth and soft. Place the ball on a flat surface and flatten it slightly at the base. Without moving the ball from the bench, roll the ball back and forward at the bottom to form a light-bulb shape (photo 1).

NOSE

The facial features for your Video nuts are up to you. The crazier, the better!

To create an 'elephant trunk' nose, roll a peanut-sized ball of coloured icing into a sausage, making one end slightly thicker than the other. It can be whatever length you wish. Trim the excess icing (photo 2).

Flatten both the ends of the trunk with your finger. Now attach the thicker end to your Video nut with a dab of water.

HAIR

The hair can be as crazy as you wish. To make a cone, roll a pea-sized ball of coloured icing into a short sausage, then roll one end to a thin point. Attach it to your Video nut with a dab of water (photo 3).

EAR

Flatten a pea-sized ball of icing between your fingers. Indent one side with your finger or a balling tool. Stick the flat side of the ear onto the head with a dab of water (photo 4).

EYES

Roll the peanut-sized ball of coloured icing into two small balls; flatten them between your fingers. Stick them to the face with a dab of water. Roll two smaller balls from the contrasting coloured icing and repeat.

For the pupils, roll two small balls from a pea-sized ball of black icing and flatten them. Using a dab of water, stick them on top of each eye to form the pupils (photo 5).

Note: You can use the eye icings to make one large eye, instead of two smaller ones.

MOUTH

Roaring open mouths: Roll the peanut-sized ball of black icing out to 2 mm (1/16 in) thick. Using a small knife, cut out any mouth shape you wish: round, oval, jellybean, square. Stick it onto the Video nut with a dab of water. To create the lips, roll the red icing into a very thin sausage, then stick it on the joining line between the mouth and the face with a dab of water.

Straight teeth: Roll your ball of white icing out to 2 mm (1/16 in) thick. Cut it into a square. Mark a line on the square to create two big teeth. Stick it onto your Video nut's mouth with a dab of water (photo 6).

Sausage teeth: Roll rice grain–sized balls of white icing into sausages. Gently press them so they have a flat back and pointy or square tips. Stick them on the mouth with a tiny dab of water.

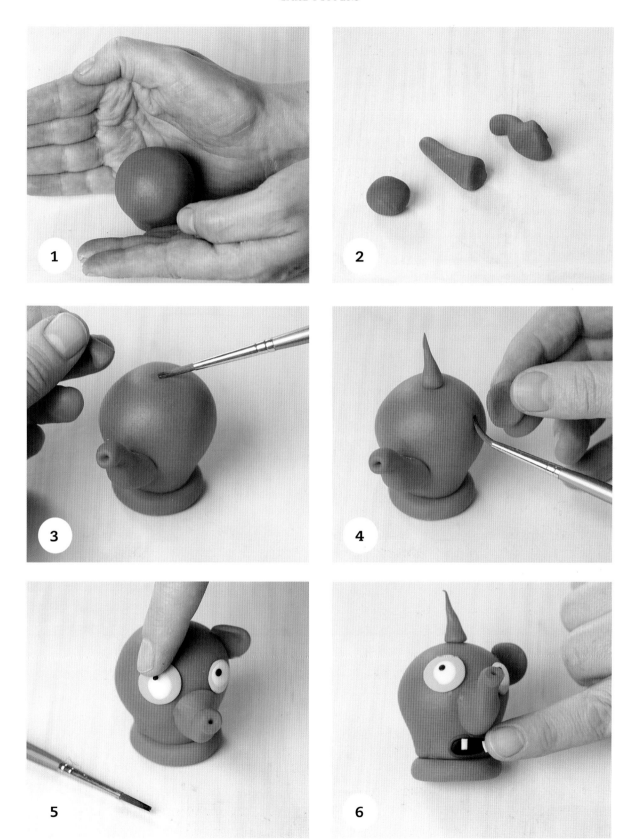

BABY DRAGON

If you were given a baby dragon, would you keep it? I have always wondered about this because I would love to own a baby dragon, but all babies grow up, and it could end up being a pet that is bigger than a bus, that also breathes fire — not to mention what it might like to eat for breakfast!

But if you love fairy tales, wizards, spells or fantasy creatures, a Baby dragon cake is the most magical gift. Now I need to tell you a bit more about this particular dragon. Red dragons like these are Chinese Fireballs — you can tell this because not only are they red, but their eggs are golden, they are usually found in the company of wizards and they have magical powers.

But then again you may want to create a different dragon. It's a difficult choice because some are easy-going and others are savages, but the good news is that all of them have fabulous talents and special abilities.

Some different dragons include the Antipodean Opal Eye, said to be the most beautiful of dragons. The Welsh Green dragon is quite calm. The Hebridean Black dragon has rough scales and brilliant purple eyes. The Hungarian HornTail, the most dangerous species, got its name from the spikes all over its tail. And the Swedish Short-Snout is a silvery-blue dragon.

If you want to give someone something magical, make them a Baby dragon. They will be so excited. Just warn them what will happen when it grows up!

EQUIPMENT
Zip-lock bag
Small kitchen knife
Medium paintbrush
Frilling tool
Styrofoam egg or chocolate Easter egg mould
Small rolling pin

MATERIALS – 1 DRAGON
Tylose
20 g ($^3/_4$ oz) red icing (body)
8 g ($^1/_6$ oz) red icing (tail)
12 g ($^1/_3$ oz) red icing (legs)
8 g ($^1/_6$ oz) red icing (arms)
50 g ($1^3/_4$ oz) red icing (head)
1 pea-sized ball of white icing (eyes)
1 pea-sized ball of black icing (eyes)
1 peanut-sized ball of red icing (wings)
1 peanut-sized ball of white icing (claws)
Dried spaghetti

WHAT YOU NEED

MATERIALS – EGG
100 g (3½ oz) white icing
    (egg shell)
Edible gold dust
Decorating alcohol

COLOUR THE FONDANT ICING

Mix the colours the day before if possible, to make intense colours easier to work with. For instructions on how to colour fondant icing, see pages 178–179.

MEASURE AND ROLL

Measure each amount of icing required per body part, then roll each into a ball. Place in a zip-lock bag so they don't dry out.

BODY

Start with the body, as this will provide the base for the rest of the dragon. Roll your 20 g (¾ oz) ball of red icing, making sure it is smooth and crack-free. Roll it between your hands to create a pear shape, then place the bottom on a flat work surface.

Now for the exciting part: pinch the back of the dragon body between your fingers, three times along the spine, to form the dragon's spikes (photo 1). Finally, use the back of your knife and indent lines across the dragon's tummy.

TAIL

Roll your 8 g (⅙ oz) ball of red icing, making sure it is smooth and crack-free. Roll the ball into a cone shape on a flat work surface. Pinch the top of the cone four times, as you did for the dragon's back to form the spikes.

Flatten the thickest end of the cone with your finger, then stick it onto the back of your dragon with a dab of water (photo 2).

LEGS

Roll your 12 g (⅓ oz) ball of red icing into a sausage. Using a sharp knife, cut the sausage on an angle in the middle. Soften at the hip joint (the angle), then stick the legs onto your dragon with a dab of water. Pinch the feet up into place with your fingers (photo 3).

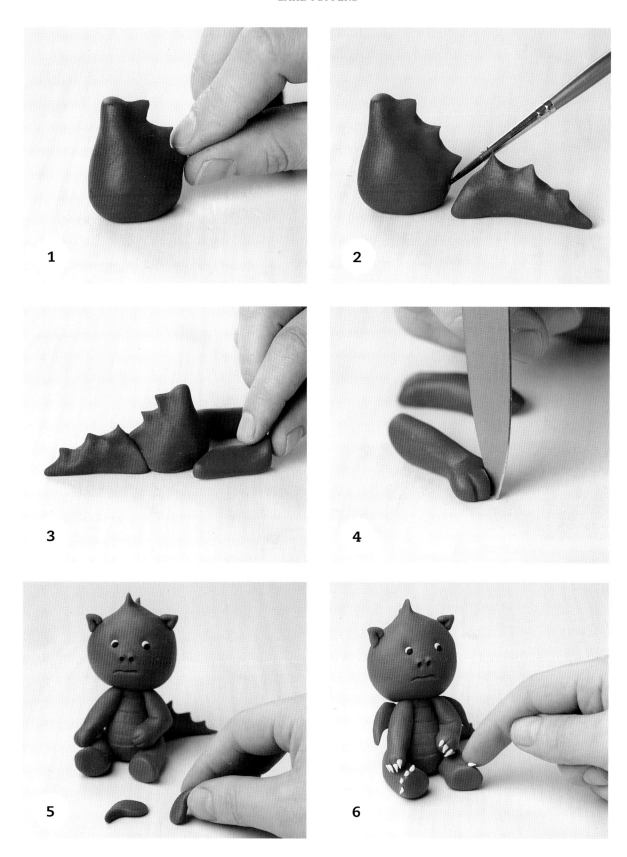

ARMS

Roll your 8 g (⅙ oz) ball of red icing into a sausage. Using a sharp knife, cut the sausage on an angle in the middle.

Using the back of your sharp knife, indent two lines at the end of each arm for the fingers (photo 4, page 101).

Stick the arms onto your dragon with a dab of water. If you'd like a bended arm, use the back of your knife to indent the elbow.

HEAD

Roll your 50 g (1¾ oz) ball of red icing, making sure it is smooth and crack-free. Place the ball on a flat work surface and flatten it slightly. Pinch five spikes along the back of the head, making sure they are the same shape and size as the spikes on the dragon's back.

Insert two 10 cm (4 in) lengths of dried spaghetti halfway into the base of the head.

Secure the head onto the dragon's body, by inserting the exposed ends of spaghetti into the body.

EYES AND FACE

Using your frilling tool or the end of a paintbrush, poke two small holes into the head for the eyes. Roll two small balls from the pea-sized ball of white icing and place them in the holes. Roll two smaller balls from the pea-sized ball of black icing and place them on top to form the pupils.

With your frilling tool, make two holes for the nose. Use the back of your sharp knife to make an indent for the mouth.

WINGS

Split the peanut-sized ball of red icing into two equal pieces. Roll each piece into a ball. Turn the balls into teardrops by gently rolling one side. Flatten each teardrop with your finger, to make little wings (photo 5, page 101). Stick them onto your dragon's back with a dab of water.

CLAWS

Split your peanut-sized ball of white icing into eight equal pieces. Split each piece in half again.

Gently roll each piece into a tiny ball, then gently pinch each one to give them pointy ends.

Carefully attach the flatter ends of the claws to the dragon's hands and feet — four claws for each hand and foot (photo 6, page 101).

DRAGON EGG

Mix the fondant icing

Mix your white icing with Tylose
(see page 93). Roll it out to about 2 mm
(1/16 in) thick.

Cut an oval

Cut the white icing into an oval shape,
to a similar shape and size as your
styrofoam egg or Easter egg mould.

Cover the mould

If using a styrofoam egg, cover half the
egg with the icing. If using a chocolate
egg mould, line the mould with the icing.
Leave to dry for at least 1 day.

Mark the edges

Once your egg shell is dry, carefully remove
it from the mould. Either leave it whole,
or break it into smaller pieces with jagged
edges (photo 1), for an egg that looks like
it has hatched a dragon.

Paint the egg

Mix your edible gold dust with decorating
alcohol (photo 2) and paint your egg shell.

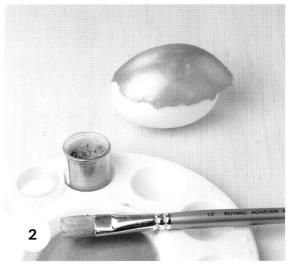

FAT RATS

If I found a rat at Planet Cake I would scream at the top of my lungs while dialling on my mobile for a rat-catcher. However, in stories, Fat rats have an extraordinary sense of smell and taste, and a love of food that has made them famous chefs the world over.

'Chef' means 'leader' in French. We use this word in English because the chef is the boss of the kitchen. Since this is a lot of work, a chef is almost always busy.

The littlest Fat rat is a pastry chef — he loves making cakes, desserts and pastries. A pastry chef makes sugar sculptures and wedding cakes and chocolate. He needs to be artistic and creative to produce cakes and desserts that look as good as they taste. All the cake makers at Planet Cake are pastry chefs.

All chefs have to wear a special uniform. The chef's tall hat has been around for hundreds of years, and hats of different heights sometimes show how important you are in a kitchen.

If someone you know dreams of becoming a chef, or is a fantastic cook, then these characters are the best ones to make. Try to include some of their favourite foods or the things they like cooking. If they are a girl chef, you might even want to add a pink bow to their chef's hat.

EQUIPMENT
Zip-lock bag
Small kitchen knife
Medium paintbrush
Frilling tool
Balling tool

MATERIALS – 1 FAT RAT
Tylose
60 g (2¼ oz) brown icing (body)
2 peanut-sized balls of brown icing (legs)
1 peanut-sized ball of pink icing
1 grape-sized ball of brown icing
1 peanut-sized ball of pink icing
20 g (¾ oz) brown icing (head)
Dried spaghetti
1 pea-sized ball of white icing
1 pea-sized ball of black icing
2 pea-sized balls of brown icing
1 pea-sized ball of pink icing
1 grape-sized ball of pink icing
20 g (¾ oz) white icing (hat)
60 g (2¼ oz) yellow icing (cheese)

COLOUR THE FONDANT ICING

Mix the colours the day before if possible, to make intense colours easier to work with. For instructions on how to colour fondant icing, see pages 178–179.

MEASURE AND ROLL

Measure each amount of icing required per body part, then roll each into a ball. Place in a zip-lock bag so they don't dry out.

BODY

Roll your 60 g (2¼ oz) ball of brown icing into a cone. Place it on a flat work surface, with the wide end on the bottom.

LEGS

Squash each peanut-sized ball of brown icing flat. Stick them on the front of the body, near the base, with a dab of water.

FEET

Cut one peanut-sized ball of pink icing in half. Roll each half into a ball. Turn each ball into a teardrop shape by gently rolling one side thinner. Flatten the teardrops with your finger to make two feet.

Using a knife, cut three toes into each foot (photo 1). Gently roll and smooth the toes with your fingers. With a dab of water, stick the feet flat on the legs. Using your fingers, fold the toes out.

ARMS

Roll your grape-sized ball of brown icing into a sausage. Using a knife, cut the sausage on an angle in the middle. Stick the arms onto your rat with a dab of water. If you'd like a bended arm, use the back of your knife to indent the elbow.

FINGERS

Cut your other peanut-sized ball of pink icing in half. Roll each half into a ball. Turn each ball into a teardrop shape by gently rolling one side thinner. Flatten the teardrops with your finger to make a hand.

Using a knife, cut four fingers into each hand. Gently roll and smooth the fingers with your fingers. With a dab of water, stick the hands flat onto the ends of the arms (photo 2).

HEAD

Roll your 20 g (¾ oz) ball of brown icing, making sure it is smooth and crack-free. Roll it into a pear shape, with a pointy end. Place it in both hands, then bend the pointy end of the pear shape up (photo 3) to form the rat's nose.

Using the back of a sharp knife, mark a line downwards at the end of the nose, and then across to form the mouth.

Insert two 5 cm (2 in) lengths of dried spaghetti halfway into the top of the body. Attach the head onto the body.

EYES

Using your frilling tool or the end of a paintbrush, poke two small holes in the head for the eyes. Roll two small balls from the pea-sized ball of white icing and place them in the holes. Roll two smaller balls from the pea-sized ball of black icing and stick them on top to form the pupils.

EARS

Shape the two pea-sized balls of brown icing into cone shapes. Flatten each one slightly, then indent with the frilling tool. Stick your ears onto the side of the head with a dab of water.

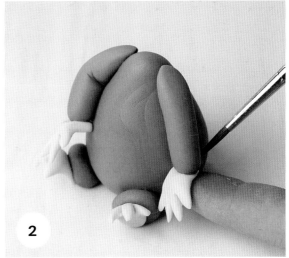

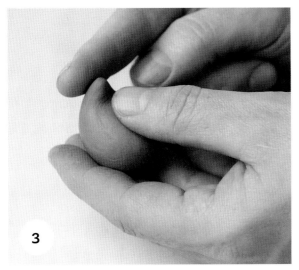

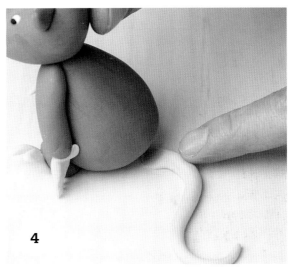

NOSE

Slightly pinch one side of the pea-sized ball of pink icing to make a nose shape. Stick the nose to the face with a dab of water.

TAIL

Roll your grape-sized ball of pink icing into a long, thin sausage. Flatten it on one end with your finger (photo 4). Stick it under the body with a dab of water. For a curled tail, wrap the tail around your little finger or a pencil or paintbrush, then gently let it go, keeping some of the curl.

HAT

Take your 20 g (¾ oz) ball of white icing and roll the bottom half backwards and forwards with your fingers, creating a tapered bottom, similar to a light bulb. Using the back of your knife, mark some lines on the top of the hat.

CHEESE

Using your fingers, shape your ball of yellow icing into a triangle. Using the small end of your balling tool, make some indents in the cheese for a Swiss-cheese effect.

HIP HOP DUDES

These guys are so cool; if you like MC rappers, hip hop music or just octopuses, then these are the toppers to make. My brother Milo would have loved these characters as a boy; he loves music, rides his skateboard everywhere and has a bit of attitude.

If you have a friend, brother or sister who you think is pretty cool, then think about changing the colour of the Hip hop dudes to match the colours they like to wear. Use your imagination and include items like skateboards, music-mixing decks and sunglasses.

What about octopuses? These are awesome animals — did you know some people keep octopuses as pets? I was a bit shocked to find out they often escape from their aquarium tanks due to their talent for solving problems and their agile bodies.

So there's a lot more to these cool characters than meets the eye. They are super smart and as tough as nails. They would be great for any lucky dudes you know — and even better, they are pretty easy to make, so use your imagination as much as possible and turn them into anything you want.

EQUIPMENT
Zip-lock bag
Small kitchen knife
Frilling tool
Medium paintbrush
Small rolling pin

MATERIALS – 1 HIP HOP DUDE
Tylose
70 g (2½ oz) coloured icing (body)
18 g (¾ oz) coloured icing (legs)
1 pea-sized ball of white icing (eyes)
1 pea-sized ball of black icing (eyes)
1 peanut-sized ball of pink icing (tongue poke; optional)
1 pea-sized ball of red icing (lips; optional)
1 pea-sized ball of white icing (teeth; optional)
1 peanut-sized ball of coloured icing (hair)

COLOUR THE FONDANT ICING

Mix the colours the day before if possible, to make intense colours easier to work with. For instructions on how to colour fondant icing, see pages 178–179.

MEASURE AND ROLL

Measure each amount of icing required per body part, then roll each into a ball. Place in a zip-lock bag so they don't dry out.

BODY

Make sure your 70 g (2½ oz) ball of coloured icing is smooth, soft and crack-free. Place on a flat work surface and flatten it slightly.

LEGS

Make sure your 18 g (¾ oz) ball of icing is smooth, soft and crack-free. Roll it into a sausage. Using a knife, cut the sausage into six even pieces. Roll each piece into a tapered sausage about 7 cm (2¾ in) long. Bend the legs if you like (photo 1). Soften each leg at the leg joint, then stick them onto your dude with a dab of water.

EYES

Using your frilling tool or the end of a paintbrush, poke two small holes in the head for the eyes (photo 2). Roll two small balls from the pea-sized ball of white icing and place them in the holes. Roll two smaller balls from the ball of black icing and stick them on top to form the pupils.

Note: You can use the eye icings to make one large eye, instead of two smaller ones.

MOUTH

Tongue poke (option 1): While the icing on the dude's face is still soft, use a frilling tool to indent the mouth and make a grimace or an 'O' shape. For the tongue, roll the peanut-sized ball of pink icing into a jellybean shape and flatten it. Cut one straight edge. Place the flat edge in the mouth using a small dab of water (photo 3).

Use a frilling tool or the back of a knife to mark the centre line on the tongue.

Lips (option 2): Roll your pea-sized ball of red icing into a thick or thin sausage, depending on how thick you want the lips to be. Using your knife or fingers, create the lip shape you want. Stick it on your dude with a dab of water.

Teeth (option 3): Roll your pea-sized ball of white icing out to 2 mm (1/16 in) thick. Using a knife, cut it into a square, then mark a line on the front of your square to create two big teeth. Stick it onto your dude with a dab of water (photo 4).

HAIR

Hair tufts (option 1): Make several small cones or a ponytail from the peanut-sized ball of coloured icing. Twist the cones or ponytail, or mark with your frilling tool, then attach to the head with a dab of water (photo 5).

You can attach a ribbon to the ponytail by making a tiny icing rectangle, squeezing it in the middle, creating an indent on your ponytail, and attaching the ribbon into the indent with a dab of water.

Hair disc (option 2): Roll your small ball of coloured icing into a smooth ball, then flatten it. Stick it onto the head with a dab of water. Make lines with the back of your knife or frilling tool to give a wavy look (photo 6).

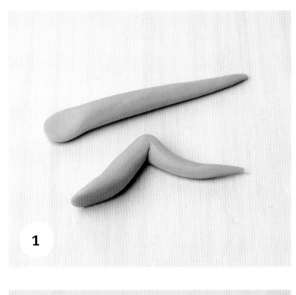

1

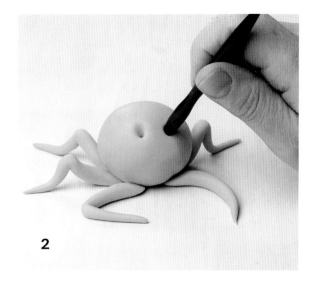

2

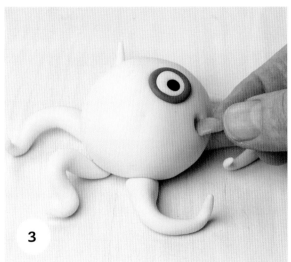

3

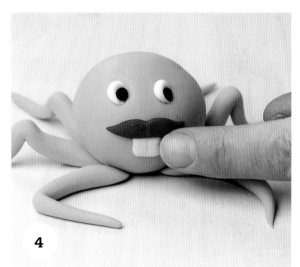

4

5

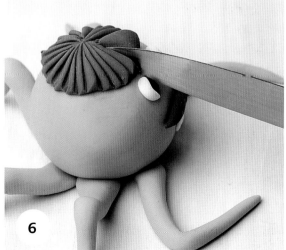

6

LITTLE NIPPER LIFESAVERS

Did you know that some kids are junior lifesavers? They are often called 'nippers' or 'little nippers', and that's why I thought there could be no better lifesavers for your cake than these crazy crustaceans.

A surf lifesaver is a trained volunteer who patrols our beaches. They have a number of very important jobs, including rescues, providing first aid and keeping an eye on the beach to make sure it is safe to swim, including sounding an alarm if they see a shark (thank goodness this very rarely happens).

Most lifesavers are very happy because they lead a fit and healthy lifestyle; they also have lots of friends, compete in surf sports, and are very popular in the local community.

If you love the beach, or know someone who does, these characters are perfect. When you give the lucky person the cake, you can remind them to always wear sunscreen — or they may end up 'as red as a lobster'!

EQUIPMENT
Zip-lock bag
Small kitchen knife
Medium paintbrush
Frilling tool
Large plastic drinking straw or piping nozzle
Toothpick
Styrofoam

MATERIALS – 1 LOBSTER
Tylose
60 g (2¼ oz) orange icing (body)
6 pea-sized balls of orange icing (legs)
2 grape-sized balls of orange icing (claws)
2 peanut-sized balls of orange icing (eyes)
1 peanut-sized ball of white icing (eyes)
1 pea-sized ball of black icing (eyes)
Dried spaghetti

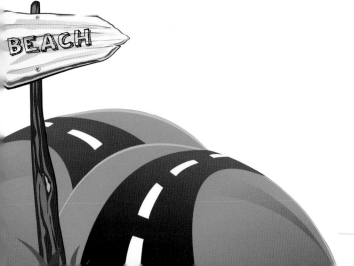

COLOUR THE FONDANT ICING

Mix the colours the day before if possible, to make intense colours easier to work with. For instructions on how to colour fondant icing, see pages 178–179.

MEASURE AND ROLL

Measure each amount of icing required per body part, then roll each into a ball. Place in a zip-lock bag so they don't dry out.

BODY

Roll the 60 g (2¼ oz) ball of orange icing into the shape of an ice-cream cone, about 9 cm (3½ in) long. Using your knife, cut up through the middle of the thinnest end of your cone, about 2 cm (¾ in) deep (photo 1). Now bend both sides of the base of the cone where you have cut, to form feet.

Using the back of your knife, mark the front of the lobster with horizontal indents, to form the belly (photo 2).

Stand your lobster upright. Place a toothpick up the centre of the lobster (to be removed later and replaced with spaghetti when you stand your lobster on the cake). Place the body on some styrofoam to dry.

LEGS

Roll your six pea-sized balls of orange icing into a teardrop shape. For a bent leg, use the back of your knife and crease the leg at the elbow. Stick the legs to the bottom half of the body with a dab of water (photo 3).

CLAWS

Roll your two grape-sized balls of orange icing into a teardrop shape, then flatten the teardrops evenly. Cut down the middle of the widest end (photo 4) and separate the claws. Stick the claws onto the top of the body with a dab of water.

MOUTH

To create the mouth, take a large plastic drinking straw or the wide end of a piping nozzle, and gently press it against the head to imprint the mouth (photo 5).

EYES

Roll the two peanut-sized balls of orange icing into smooth balls. Using your frilling tool, make a hole in each one. Roll two balls from the peanut-sized ball of white icing and flatten them between your fingers. Place them in your orange eyeball sockets.

Roll two smaller balls from the pea-sized of black icing and flatten them between your fingers. Stick them on the white balls with a dab of water (photo 6) — the crazier the better!

Stick the eyes onto the lobster's head with a dab of water.

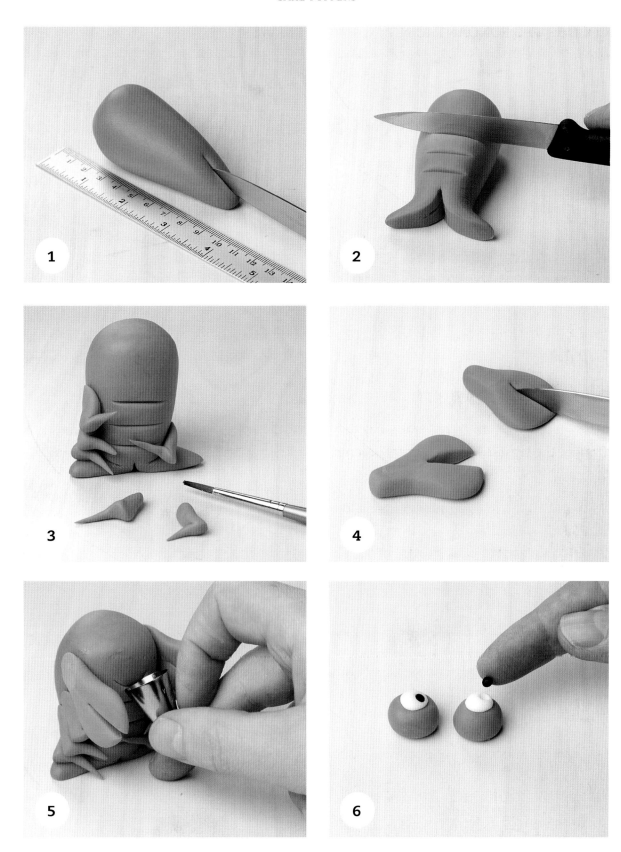

MR DONUT & FRIENDS

How would you feel if you were a donut and knew that you were about to be eaten? Pretty scared, I would imagine! But if you were a donut cake topper with a great personality like Mr Donut, then chances are that people would like you to hang around for the party!

These cake toppers are perfect for anyone who loves food. My Dad LOVES hamburgers, so this is where the idea for Harry the Hamburger came from. I love hot dogs, so I put these on the cake as well.

If you are making your favourite food as a cake topper, think about what type of personality it would have. For example, I think a donut would always be telling jokes and laughing a lot, and a hot dog would probably love sport, because they are always hanging out at sports events — and a hamburger would love to shop, because I often find I eat hamburgers at shopping centres.

These toppers are so much fun and will make people smile. They are perfect for the ultimate birthday cake. Think about it: cake, donut, hamburgers and hot dogs… all the things you love on one cake!

EQUIPMENT
Small kitchen knife
Medium paintbrush
Zip-lock bag
Frilling tool
Circle cutter
Palette knife
Piping bag and nozzle
Small rolling pin

MATERIALS – 1 DONUT
Tylose
50 g (1¾ oz) light brown icing (donut)
Royal icing (donut glaze), in your favourite colour
Hundreds and thousands (decoration)
2 x 5 g (⅛ oz) balls of black icing (feet)
2 pea-sized balls of white icing (eyes)
1 pea-sized ball of black icing (eyes)

WHAT YOU NEED

MATERIALS – 1 HOT DOG
60 g (2¼ oz) light brown icing (bun)

25 g (1 oz) dark pink icing (sausage)

10 g (¼ oz) red icing (sauce)

2 x 5 g (⅛ oz) balls of black icing (feet)

2 pea-sized balls of white icing (eyes)

1 pea-sized ball of black icing (eyes)

MATERIALS – 1 HAMBURGER
2 x 30 g (1 oz) balls of light brown icing (bun)

12 g (⅓ oz) red icing (tomato)

12 g (⅓ oz) green icing (lettuce)

12 g (⅓ oz) brown icing (meat)

1 peanut-sized ball of white icing (teeth)

1 pea-sized ball of white icing (eyes)

1 pea-sized ball of black icing (eyes)

10 g (¼ oz) red icing (cap)

2 x 5 g (⅛ oz) black icing (feet)

DONUT
Colour the fondant icing: Mix the colours the day before if possible, to make intense colours easier to work with. For instructions on how to colour fondant icing, see pages 178–179.

Measure and roll: Measure each amount of icing required per body part, then roll each into a ball. Place in a zip-lock bag so they don't dry out.

Donut: Roll your 50 g (1¾ oz) ball of light brown icing, making sure it is soft, smooth and crack-free. Place the ball on a flat surface and flatten it to the thickness you wish your donut to be. Poke a hole through the middle of the donut and keep smoothing around the inside until you have a perfectly smooth donut shape (photo 1). Allow to dry.

Glaze: Mix and colour your royal icing. To do this, add the food colour in very small quantities and mix together with a palette knife, on a board or plate. Don't make the colour too dark as it will darken when it dries.

Either pipe the icing onto your donut, or smooth it on with a palette knife. While the royal icing is still wet, sprinkle hundreds and thousands on top. Allow to dry.

Feet: Roll your two 5 g (⅛ oz) balls of black icing into oval shapes, gently flattening each ball. Now flatten one end of each oval with your finger, to make an indent to fit under the body (photo 2). Stick the feet underneath the body with a dab of water. Pinch the feet into place with your fingers.

Eyes: Lightly flatten both pea-sized balls of white icing. Using your frilling tool, make a hole in each one. Roll your pea-sized ball of black icing into two small balls and place them in the eyeball sockets. The crazier the better! Stick the eyes onto your donut with a dab of water (photo 3). Allow to dry.

1

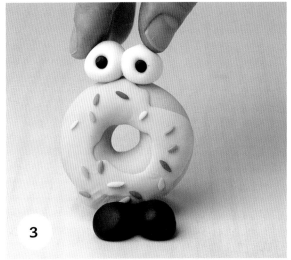

3

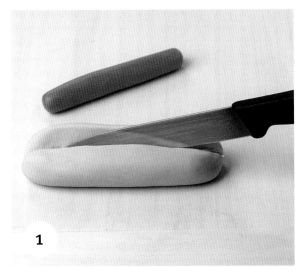

1

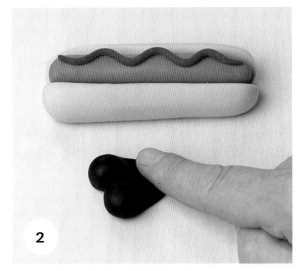

2

HOT DOG
Colour the fondant icing: Mix the colours the day before if possible, to make intense colours easier to work with. For instructions on how to colour fondant icing, see pages 178–179.

Measure and roll: Measure each amount of icing required per body part, then roll each into a ball. Place in a zip-lock bag so they don't dry out.

Bun: Roll your 60 g (2¼ oz) ball of light brown icing into a thick sausage. Split the sausage down one side with a sharp knife, then open it out like a bun (photo 1).

Sausage: Roll your ball of dark pink icing into a sausage, slightly shorter than your 'bun'. Place your 'sausage' in the bun, securing it with a dab of water.

Sauce: Roll your ball of red icing into a thin sausage. Place it on the sausage to look like a drizzle of sauce, securing it with a dab of water. Trim the ends with a knife.

Feet: Roll your two 5 g (1/8 oz) balls of black icing into oval shapes by gently flattening each ball. Flatten one end of each oval with your finger, to make an indent to fit under the body (photo 2, page 119). Stick them underneath the body with a dab of water. Pinch the feet into place with your fingers.

Eyes: Lightly flatten your two balls of white icing. Using a frilling tool, make a hole in each. Roll your pea-sized ball of black icing into two smaller balls and place them in the eyeball sockets. Stick the eyes onto your hot dog with a dab of water. Allow to dry.

HAMBURGER
Colour the fondant icing: Mix the colours the day before if possible, to make intense colours easier to work with. For instructions on colouring fondant icing, see pages 178–179.

Measure and roll: Measure each amount of icing required per body part, then roll each into a ball. Place in a zip-lock bag so they don't dry out.

Buns: Roll your two 30 g (1 oz) balls of light brown icing, making sure they are soft, smooth and crack-free. Place on a flat work surface and flatten each with the palm of your hand to make two bun halves. Turn one of them over to form the base bun half.

Tomato and lettuce: Roll out your ball of red icing to 2 mm (1/16 in) thick, then your ball of green icing. Using a circle cutter, cut out two circles from each piece of coloured icing, then cut each circle in half. Place them alternately on your bun base, securing them with a dab of water, to form your layers of tomato and lettuce (photo 1, opposite).

Meat: Roll out your 12 g (1/3 oz) ball of brown icing to 5 mm (1/4 in) thick and cut out a circle using a circle cutter. (Or roll the icing to a smooth ball and flatten it to 5 mm/1/4 in thick.) Place it on top of the lettuce and tomato to form the meat patty, securing it with a dab of water.

Place the other bun half on top of the meat patty, securing it with a dab of water.

Mouth and teeth: With the edge of your circle cutter, indent a smile shape on the top of the burger (photo 2). Make two dimple marks at each end of the smile with your frilling tool.

Roll the peanut-sized ball of white icing out to 2 mm (1/16 in) thick. Using a knife, cut out a mouth shape and place it in the smile gap, securing it with a dab of water.

Now indent some teeth with the back of your knife.

Eyes: Using your frilling tool or the end of a paintbrush, poke two small holes for the eyes on the top of your top hamburger bun (photo 3). Roll your pea-sized ball of white icing into two small balls and place them in the holes. Roll two smaller balls from the pea-sized ball of black icing and place on top to form the pupils.

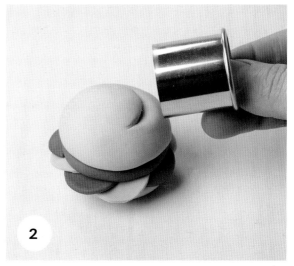

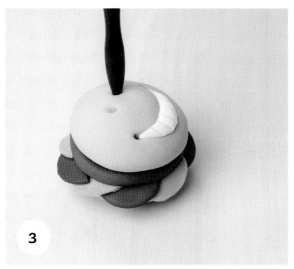

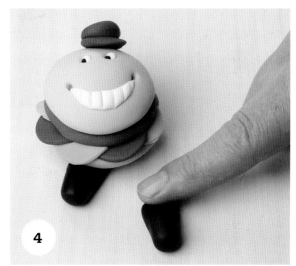

Cap: Lightly flatten your 10 g (¼ oz) ball of red icing. Place on a flat work surface and squash down one-quarter of the flattened ball to form the rim of the cap. Mark a cap indent around the front with a knife. Stick the cap onto the burger with a dab of water.

Feet: Roll your two 5 g (⅛ oz) balls of black icing into oval shapes by gently flattening each ball. Flatten one end of each oval with your finger, to make an indent to fit under the body (photo 4). Stick them underneath the body with a dab of water. Pinch the feet into place with your fingers.

MRS ZUCKER'S BITS & PIECES

My best friend Melanie gets a real kick out of scaring me. Sometimes she hides behind a door and jumps out when I least expect it. She makes weird scary noises at night to freak me out and she loves to tell super-scary ghost stories. The really shocking thing about this behaviour is that Melanie is a grown-up!

The best thing about getting a fright from a friend is how funny it is. That's why Melanie scares me — so she can watch me jump ten feet into the air and then we both burst out laughing.

So if you want to scare your friends, make some of Mrs Zucker's bits & pieces and place them on a gruesome cake. You could make it even scarier by baking a red velvet cake (see page 25), which is bright red. Try playing a trick on your friends by nibbling on a finger or eyeball when they come to look at your creation — your guests will be so grossed out they may not be able to eat the cake!

The only thing you need to remember is that younger kids and babies could get truly frightened, so make sure you let them know it is just a cake.

These cake toppers are dead easy (excuse the pun) to make. If you match them with our red velvet cake it will be the highlight of any horror or Halloween party.

EQUIPMENT
Zip-lock bag
Small kitchen knife
Balling tool
Frilling tool
Fine paintbrush

MATERIALS – 1 FINGER
Tylose
20 g (¾ oz) light green icing
1 pea-sized ball of red or black icing

MATERIALS – 1 EYEBALL
15 g (½ oz) white icing
1 pea-sized ball of blue icing
1 pea-sized ball of black icing
10 g (¼ oz) red icing
Red colour paste
Decorating alcohol

MATERIALS – 1 HAND
50 g (1³/₄ oz) green icing
1 pea-sized ball of red or black icing
Dried spaghetti

MATERIALS – 1 BONE
25 g (1 oz) white icing

MATERIALS – 1 DOGGY DOO
25 g (1 oz) brown icing

COLOUR THE FONDANT ICING

Mix the colours the day before if possible, to make intense colours easier to work with. For instructions on how to colour fondant icing, see pages 178–179.

MEASURE AND ROLL

Measure each amount of icing required per body part, then roll each into a ball. Place in a zip-lock bag so they don't dry out.

FINGER

Roll your ball of light green icing into a sausage, then taper it slightly at one end. Using your finger, indent the tapered end to create a fingernail (photo 1).

To make the fingernail, lightly flatten the pea-sized ball of red or black icing into an oval shape. Attach it to the finger with a dab of water. Using the back of a knife, make creases across the top of the finger.

Bend the finger by placing the back of the knife underneath the 'knuckle' and indent it (photo 2).

EYEBALL

Indent your ball of white icing with the small end of a balling tool. Flatten the pea-sized ball of blue icing and place it in the indentation, securing it with a dab of water.

Using a frilling tool, make an indentation in the blue icing for the pupil. Place the ball of black icing in the hollow, securing it with a dab of water.

Lightly roll the entire ball on a flat surface to make sure all the icing colours meld together.

Roll the ball of red icing into a long sausage, thicker at one end. Twist the sausage and attach the thicker end to the back of the eyeball with a dab of water (photo 3). Mix together some red colour paste and decorating alcohol. Using a fine paintbrush, paint squiggly red lines on your eyeball, to make it look blood-shot.

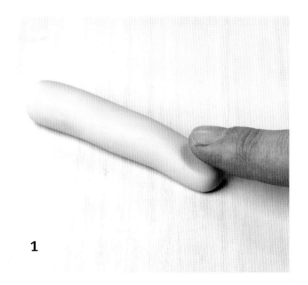

1

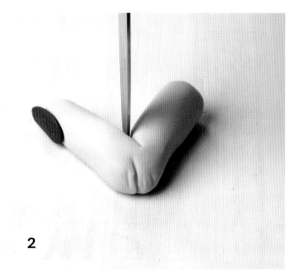

2

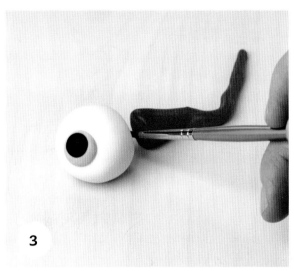

3

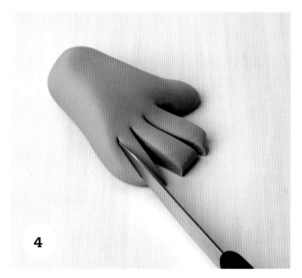

4

HAND

Roll your ball of green icing into a cylinder shape. Flatten the cylinder at one end.

Using a sharp knife, cut a thick thumb and four fingers into the thinner end of the hand (photo 4), then smooth and shape the hand with your fingers. Indent the fingernails using your finger.

To make the fingernails, roll the pea-sized ball of red or black icing into five oval shapes and lightly flatten them. Attach them to the fingers with a dab of water.

Using the back of a knife, make creases over the fingers and thumb. Place two small pieces of dried spaghetti underneath the hand, to place it on top of a cake.

BONE

Roll your ball of white icing into a long, thin cylinder. Flatten it with your hand, then indent both ends with your finger. Indent it lengthways along the 'bone'.

DOGGY DOO

Roll your ball of brown icing into a sausage, then twist it into a coil shape.

SNOW-SURFING PENGUINS

There are so many things I love about penguins. I also love snowboarding, so I thought I would bring them together with these cool figurines.

If you are like me and love snowboarding, then you know how exciting it is! I love it from when I first strap on my board. Once I get off the chairlift and start surfing the snow, I am on cloud nine. The sensation of going fast down a hill is thrilling. I love dodging trees, avoiding bad snow, riding through powder, hitting jumps, and taking new paths every run ... AWESOME!

But I also love all the friends and laughter that snowboarding brings. It is great meeting new people, pushing your limits, doing dares and double dares, listening to music and then more snowboarding. As soon as I come home I am thinking about the next time I can go — and how I can make it even better!

EQUIPMENT
Zip-lock bag
Small kitchen knife
Medium paintbrush
Small rolling pin

MATERIALS – 1 PENGUIN
Tylose
20 g (³/₄ oz) aqua or other coloured icing (body)
2 pea-sized balls of yellow icing (feet)
1 peanut-sized ball of white icing (tummy)
2 pea-sized balls of aqua or other coloured icing (wings)
50 g (1³/₄ oz) aqua or other coloured icing (head)
Dried spaghetti
1 pea-sized ball of yellow or orange icing (beak)
1 pea-sized ball of white icing (eyes)
1 pea-sized ball of black icing (eyes)

COLOUR THE FONDANT ICING

Mix the colours the day before if possible, to make intense colours easier to work with. For instructions on how to colour fondant icing, see pages 178–179.

MEASURE AND ROLL

Measure each amount of icing required per body part, then roll each into a ball. Place in a zip-lock bag so they don't dry out.

BODY

Roll your 20 g (¾ oz) ball of aqua icing into a cone shape. Place the wide end down on a flat work surface (photo 1).

FEET

Roll your two pea-sized balls of yellow icing into teardrops, by gently rolling one side thinner. Flatten the teardrops with your finger. Lightly indent each foot three times, to make a webbed effect (photo 2).

Stick the feet underneath the body with a dab of water. Pinch the feet up into place with your fingers.

TUMMY

Roll your peanut-sized ball of white icing out to 2 mm (¹⁄₁₆ in) thick. Using a knife, trim it into an oval shape. Stick it onto the front of the body with a dab of water.

WINGS

Like the feet, roll your two pea-sized balls of aqua icing into teardrops, by gently rolling one side thinner (photo 3). Flatten the teardrops with your finger. Attach the fat end of the teardrop on each side of the body with a dab of water. Using your fingers, gently lift the pointy end of each teardrop, to make them look like wings.

HEAD

Roll your 50 g (1¾ oz) ball of aqua icing, making sure it is soft, crack-free and a perfect round shape. Place the ball in the palm of your dry, clean hand. Now place your other hand over the top as though you are about to clap. Gently and evenly press down on the ball with both hands, to make it flatter (photo 4).

Insert two 3 cm (1¼ in) lengths of dried spaghetti halfway into the base of the head. Secure the head onto the penguin's body, by inserting the exposed ends of spaghetti into the body.

BEAK

Roll your pea-sized ball of yellow or orange icing out to 3 mm (¹⁄₈ in) thick. Using a knife, cut a small diamond shape from the icing. Place the back of your knife gently in the middle of your diamond (the thickest part). Bend the diamond in half over your knife, to form the beak (photo 5). Stick it onto the face with a dab of water.

EYES

Roll two small balls from the pea-sized ball of white icing, then flatten each one between your fingers. Stick them to your penguin's face with a dab of water.

Roll two smaller balls from your pea-sized ball of black icing and slightly flatten them. Stick them on top of the white balls with a dab of water to form the pupils (photo 6).

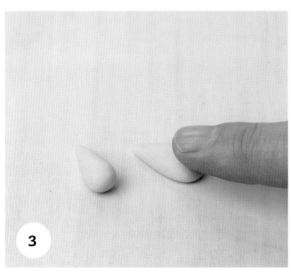

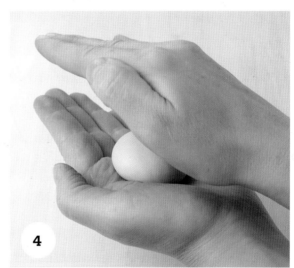

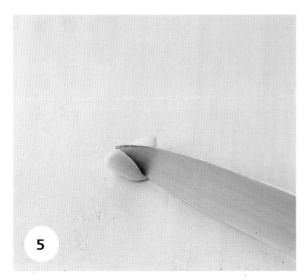

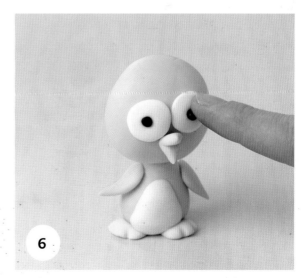

PIG & PEPPER

My Aunt Diana is one of the sweetest people on this earth; she is a nurse and looks after loads of kids all day long — and then when she gets home, she has to look after her 14 pets! She takes in all sorts of animals. Unfortunately they are usually pets that no one else wants.

All the animals adore her and they each have a special story to tell. She has a one-legged rooster that follows her everywhere and thinks he is a dog, two peach-faced parrots that have no feathers and have to wear jumpers she has knitted for them, a donkey, a dog that has lost her hearing, and a very naughty cockatoo that swears so much she has to keep him out the back.

All of Aunt Diana's pets are really funny and you would love to hear about all of them, but these cake topper characters were inspired by a very special friendship between two of her pets: a cat called Pepper, and a pot-bellied pig called Piggy. The cat and pig are inseparable and spend every day sunbaking together on Aunt Diana's back porch.

Pepper rests his head on Piggy like a pillow, and they both go to sleep. They eat together, chase the dogs together, tease the birds — and if they could, I am sure they would get married as they love each other so much.

So these cake toppers are for anyone who is getting married, has a best friend, or just loves cats and pigs. Oink, oink, meow!

EQUIPMENT
Small kitchen knife
Medium paintbrush
Zip-lock bag
Frilling tool
Small rolling pin

MATERIALS – 1 PIG
Tylose
20 g (³/₄ oz) pink icing (body)
2 pea-sized balls of pink icing (feet)
2 pea-sized balls of pink icing (arms)
50 g (1³/₄ oz) pink icing (head)
Dried spaghetti
White chiffon ribbon (veil; optional)
1 peanut-sized ball of dark pink icing (snout)
2 pea-sized balls of pink icing (ears)
1 pea-sized ball of white icing (eyes)
1 pea-sized ball of black icing (eyes)
1 peanut-sized ball of pink icing (tail)

MATERIALS – 1 PEPPER

Tylose

20 g (¾ oz) black icing (body)

1 peanut-sized ball of white icing (tummy)

2 pea-sized balls of black icing (paws)

2 pea-sized balls of white icing (paws)

50 g (1¾ oz) black icing (head)

Dried spaghetti

2 pea-sized balls of black icing (ears)

2 pea-sized balls of pink icing (ears)

1 pea-sized ball of white or pink icing (eyes)

1 pea-sized ball of black icing (eyes)

2 pea-sized balls of white icing (whisker cheeks)

1 pea-sized ball of pink icing (nose)

1 peanut-sized ball of black icing (tail)

PIG

Colour the fondant icing: Mix the colours the day before if possible, to make intense colours easier to work with. For instructions on how to colour fondant icing, see pages 178–179.

Measure and roll: Measure each amount of icing required per body part, then roll each into a ball. Place in a zip-lock bag so they don't dry out.

Body: Roll your 20 g (¾ oz) ball of pink icing into a cone. Place the wide end down on a flat surface.

Feet: Roll two pea-sized balls of pink icing into teardrops by gently rolling one side thinner. Flatten each teardrop with your finger to make two trotter feet. With the back of a knife, make a small cut in the fat end of each teardrop (photo 1), to make trotter hooves. Secure them under the body with a dab of water. Pinch the trotter up into place with your fingers.

Arms: Roll two pea-sized balls of pink icing into teardrops. With the back of a knife, make a small cut in the fat end of each teardrop, to make trotter hooves. Stick them to the body with a dab of water.

Head: Roll your 50 g (1¾ oz) ball of pink icing, making sure it is soft, crack-free and a perfect round shape. Place the ball in the palm of your dry, clean hand. Place your other hand over the top as though you are about to clap. Gently and evenly press down on the ball with both hands, to make it flatter.

Insert two 3 cm (1¼ in) lengths of dried spaghetti halfway into the base of the head. Insert the exposed ends of spaghetti into the body to secure the head. Attach the chiffon ribbon to the head, if you'd like your pig to wear a wedding veil.

Snout: Squash your peanut-sized ball of dark pink icing between your fingers to make a snout — it looks better when it's slightly oval (photo 2). Stick it onto your pig's face with a dab of water. Using your frilling tool or the end of a paintbrush, make two holes for nostrils (photo 3).

Ears: Roll two pea-sized balls of pink icing into a cone shape. Flatten each slightly and indent with the frilling tool. Stick your ears on with a dab of water.

Eyes: Using your frilling tool or the end of a paintbrush, poke two small holes into the face for the eyes. Roll your ball of white icing into two small balls and place them in the holes. Roll two smaller balls from the black icing and place on top for the pupils.

Tail: Roll your peanut-sized ball of pink icing into a long, thin sausage. Flatten one end with your finger, then stick it under the body with a dab of water. For a curly tail, wrap the tail around your little finger, then gently let it go, keeping some of the curl.

PEPPER

Colour the fondant icing: Mix the colours the day before if possible, to make intense colours easier to work with. For instructions on how to colour fondant icing, see pages 178–179.

Measure and roll: Measure each amount of icing required per body part, then roll each into a ball. Place in a zip-lock bag so they don't dry out.

Body: Roll your 20 g (¾ oz) ball of black icing into a cone (photo 1, page 135). Place the wide end down on a flat surface.

Tummy: Roll your peanut-sized ball of white icing out to 2 mm (¹⁄₁₆ in) thick. Using

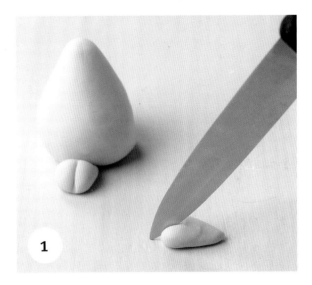

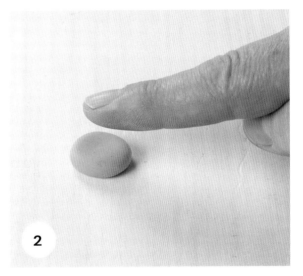

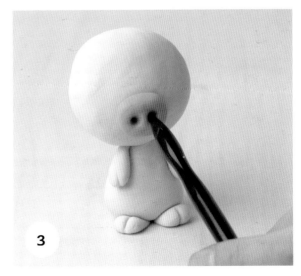

a knife, trim it into an oval shape. Stick it onto the body with a dab of water.

Paws: Split the two pea-sized balls of black icing and the two pea-sized balls of white icing in half — you will have four black and four white balls of icing.

Stick a white ball to a black ball with a dab of water. Repeat with the remaining balls, so that you have four black and white balls (photo 2).

Turn your balls into teardrop shapes by gently rolling the black side thinner (photo 3). Flatten the teardrops with your finger to make a paw. Using the back of a knife, make toe indentations on the top of the paws.

Stick two paws underneath the body for the feet, and two paws on the sides of the cat for its arms, securing each one with a dab of water. Pinch the paws into place with your fingers.

Head: Roll your 50 g (1¾ oz) ball of black icing, making sure it is soft, crack-free and a perfect round shape. Place the ball in the palm of your dry, clean hand. Now place your other hand over the top as though you are about to clap. Gently and evenly press down on the ball with both hands, to make it flatter.

Insert two 3 cm (1¼ in) lengths of dried spaghetti halfway into the base of the head. Secure the head onto the body, by inserting the exposed ends of spaghetti into the body.

Ears: Roll two pea-sized balls of black icing into a cone shape. Flatten each slightly and indent with the frilling tool.

Roll two pea-sized balls of pink icing into a cone shape, slightly smaller than the black cones. Stick them in the indentation

with a dab of water (photo 4). Now stick your ears onto the head with a dab of water.

Mouth: Using your frilling tool or the end of a paintbrush, make a hole where the mouth should be, in the bottom third of the head. Once you have made the hole and before you take your tool out, stretch the hole down slightly to make the hole bigger (photo 5).

Eyes: Using your frilling tool or the end of a paintbrush, poke two small holes in the head for the eyes. Roll a pea-sized ball of white or pink icing into two small balls and place them in the holes (photo 6). Roll two smaller balls from the black icing and place on top to form the pupils.

Whisker cheeks: Roll another two pea-sized balls of white icing into smooth balls. Squash the balls gently between your fingers to make the whisker cheeks you want. Stick them onto the front of the cat's face, on each side of the mouth, with a dab of water. Using your frilling tool or a piece of spaghetti, mark some whisker holes.

Nose: Roll another pea-sized ball of pink icing, then pinch it slightly to form a little triangle (just like a cat's nose). Stick the nose between the whisker cheeks with a dab of water.

Tail: Roll your peanut-sized ball of black icing into a long, thin sausage, then flatten on one end with your finger. Stick that end under the body with a dab of water.

For a curled tail, wrap the tail around your little finger or a pencil or paintbrush, then gently let it go, keeping some of the curl.

SOFTIE BEARS

My daughter, Estelle, loves soft toys. In fact she has so many that sometimes when I check on her after she has gone to bed, I cannot see her because she is buried under a pile of rabbits, teddy bears and other softies.

I think the loveliest thing about soft toys is that they are so velvety and cute, they are always there to give you a cuddle, and they are caring toys that always love you. If you like soft toys then you will adore these cute toppers, which are based on three of Estelle's favourite bears.

I encourage you to turn your toppers into your own favourite softies. Give them names, and make sure the cake you choose for them is filled with lots of rainbows and clouds to jump on. Softies belong in a magical kingdom that is always happy.

This cake is perfect for little children and babies, as they just love teddy bears. You could recreate their favourite teddy just by changing the colours and pattern of these ones.

If the cake is for someone older, their teddy may be looking very well loved, or maybe even a bit old and saggy! There would be nothing nicer than to include all of these things in your topper — maybe a torn ear or a missing nose. This will make the cake even more special for them.

EQUIPMENT
Small kitchen knife
Medium paintbrush
Zip-lock bag
Frilling tool

MATERIALS – 1 SOFTIE BEAR
Tylose
20 g (³/₄ oz) coloured icing (body)
1 peanut-sized ball of coloured icing (legs)
1 peanut-sized ball of coloured icing (arms)
50 g (1³/₄ oz) coloured icing (head)
Dried spaghetti
1 peanut-sized ball of coloured icing (ears)
1 pea-sized ball of contrasting coloured icing (ears; optional)
1 pea-sized ball of black icing (eyes)
1 peanut-sized ball of coloured icing (panda eyes; optional)
1 pea-sized ball of white icing (panda eyes; optional)
1 pea-sized ball of contrasting coloured icing (nose)

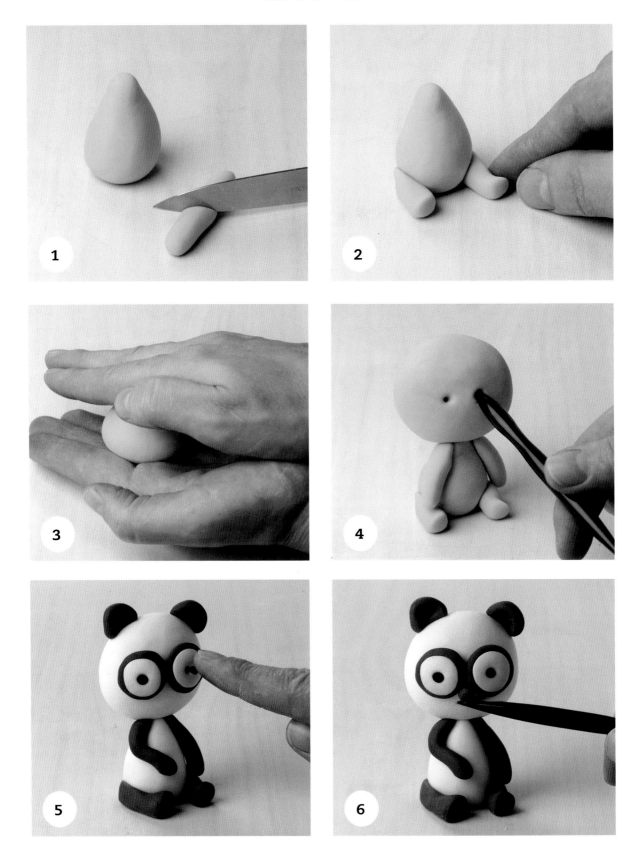

COLOUR THE FONDANT ICING

Mix the colours the day before if possible, to make intense colours easier to work with. For instructions on how to colour fondant icing, see pages 178–179.

MEASURE AND ROLL

Measure each amount of icing required per body part, then roll each into a ball. Place in a zip-lock bag so they don't dry out.

BODY

Roll your 20 g (¾ oz) ball of coloured icing into a cone shape (photo 1). Place the wide end down on a flat surface.

LEGS

Roll a peanut-sized ball of coloured icing into a sausage. Using a knife, cut the sausage on an angle in the middle (photo 1). Soften at the hip joint (the angle), then stick each leg onto the bear with a dab of water. Pinch the feet up into place with your fingers (photo 2).

ARMS

Roll another peanut-sized ball of coloured icing into a sausage. Using a knife, cut the sausage on an angle in the middle, then stick each one onto your bear with a dab of water. For a bended arm, use the back of the knife to indent each elbow.

HEAD

Roll your 50 g (1¾ oz) ball of coloured icing, making sure it is soft, crack-free and a perfect round shape. Place the ball in the palm of your dry, clean hand. Now place your other hand over the top as though you are about to clap. Gently and evenly press down on the ball with both hands, to make it flatter (photo 3).

Insert two 3 cm (1¼ in) lengths of dried spaghetti halfway into the base of the head. Secure the head onto the body, by inserting the exposed ends of spaghetti into the body.

EARS

Slightly flatten another peanut-sized ball of coloured icing into a circle shape. If you like, roll a pea-sized ball of contrasting coloured icing, slightly flatten it, then place it into the centre of the first flattened ball with a dab of water. Cut the circle in half, through the middle of the centre colour, to give you two ears. Stick the ears into position with a dab of water.

Note: You can also make koala ears, by marking little ragged lines around the ears.

EYES

Using your frilling tool or the end of a paintbrush, poke two small holes in the head for the eyes (photo 4). Roll two small balls from the pea-sized ball of black icing and place them in the holes.

Panda eyes (optional): Roll half the coloured icing into two small balls and flatten them between your fingers. Stick them onto your bear's face with a dab of water. Roll two smaller balls from the white icing and repeat the process. To form the pupils, roll two smaller balls out of the remaining coloured icing and flatten these. Stick them with a dab of water and place on top of the white eyes (photo 5).

NOSE AND MOUTH

Roll the last pea-sized ball of coloured icing into a nose shape. Stick it onto the face with a dab of water. Make an indent for the mouth beneath the nose (photo 6).

THE STOMPERS

The Planet Cake office is in a building that sits below another company. Every day the people upstairs stomp around with such heavy feet and create such a racket that we have nicknamed them the Stompers. Some days it sounds as though there is a herd of elephants up there and we cannot hear ourselves think. The floorboards creak and sometimes we hear what we call a 'stomper rush' as someone runs across the floorboards above us.

However, stompers are not unusual. I was a bit of a stomper when I was little. It doesn't just relate to how people walk — I think a Stomper is more about attitude.

One of my favourite little Stompers is Hudson, who is three years old. Not only does he stomp, but he eats sand, dresses up as Spiderman (although he forgets to put any pants on) and he is very busy annoying his older brother, Charlie, and getting into everyone's business. He is definitely a Stomper!

For Hudson's next birthday I am going to make him a Stomper cake. I think I should also make one for the office upstairs!

EQUIPMENT
Small kitchen knife
Medium paintbrush
Zip-lock bag
Frilling tool

MATERIALS – 1 STOMPER
Tylose
50 g (1¾ oz) coloured icing (body)
10 g (¼ oz) coloured icing (arms)
30 g (1 oz) coloured icing (head)
Dried spaghetti
5 g (⅛ oz) contrasting coloured icing (face)
1 pea-sized ball of contrasting coloured icing (nose)
5 g (⅛ oz) contrasting coloured icing (eyes)
1 pea-sized ball of black icing (eyes)
2 peanut-sized balls of black icing (ears)
1 pea-sized ball of red icing (heart)

COLOUR THE FONDANT ICING

Mix the colours the day before if possible, to make intense colours easier to work with. For instructions on how to colour fondant icing, see pages 178–179.

MEASURE AND ROLL

Measure each amount of icing required per body part, then roll each into a ball. Place in a zip-lock bag so they don't dry out.

BODY

Roll your 50 g (1¾ oz) ball of coloured icing into a cylinder shape. Lay it down, on a flat surface. Using your hand, press the cylinder flat. Using a knife, cut a straight line into the bottom of the cylinder for the legs. Bend the legs into position, leaving the Stomper lying down. Use the back of the knife or a frilling tool to mark the top of the thigh crease, so it will look like a 'Y' (photo 1). Shape the feet by bending them out a little.

ARMS

Roll your 10 g (¼ oz) ball of coloured icing into a sausage. Using a knife, cut the sausage on an angle in the middle. Leaving the Stomper lying down, stick the arms onto the sides with a dab of water (photo 2). For a bended arm, use the back of a knife to indent the elbow.

HEAD

Roll your 30 g (1 oz) ball of coloured icing, making sure it is soft, crack-free and a perfect round shape. Place the ball in the palm of your dry, clean hand. Now place your other hand over the top as though you are about to clap. Gently and evenly press down on the ball with both hands, to make it flatter (photo 3).

FACE

Squash the 5 g (⅛ oz) ball of contrasting coloured icing flat. Stick it onto the face with a dab of water (photo 4). Use the back of a knife to mark an indent for the mouth.

NOSE

Gently squash your pea-sized ball of coloured icing to form an oval shape. Stick the nose onto the face with a dab of water.

EYES

Make these as crazy as you like. Split the 5 g (⅛ oz) ball of contrasting coloured icing in half and roll into one or two small balls. Flatten the ball or balls between your fingers, then attach to your Stomper's face with a dab of water.

Roll two small balls from the pea-sized ball of black icing. Place them on the eyes or face to form the pupils, securing them with a dab of water (photo 5).

Insert two 3 cm (1¼ in) lengths of dried spaghetti halfway into the base of the head. Leaving the Stomper lying down, secure the head onto the body, by inserting the exposed ends of spaghetti into the body.

Dry the Stomper lying down.

EARS

Roll your two peanut-sized balls of black icing into small cones. Flatten the base of the wide end. Stick the base of the wide end on the top of the Stomper's head with a dab of water. Using your fingers, slightly curve the ears to look like horns (photo 6).

HEART

Roll the red icing into a teardrop shape and gently flatten. Mark a little groove in the top. Stick it onto the chest with a dab of water.

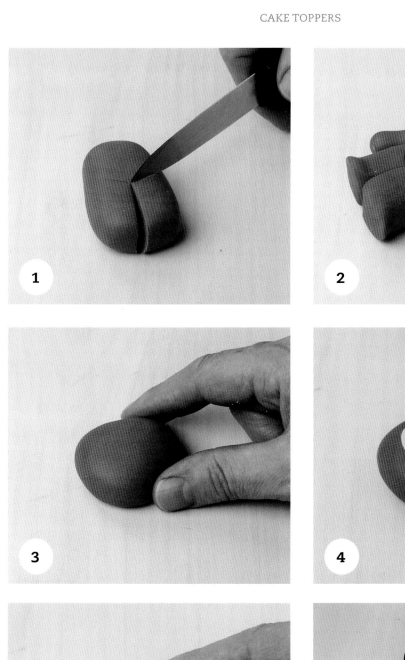

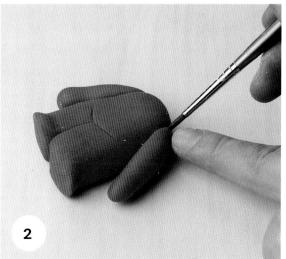

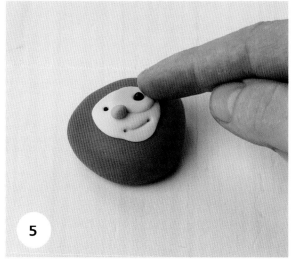

NINJA RABBITS

At Planet Cake we have a cake decorator named Jess. When she is not making cakes, Jess is a kick-boxing champion! That's pretty strange for a cake shop, but she really is our very own Ninja, and she inspired me to create these bunnies.

Two Ninja rabbits challenge each other in a bunny showdown. They are quick, agile and they act like ninjas. Are these rabbits fighting over cake, or maybe they are fighting for carrots? Rabbits, like ninjas, have lightning speed, dexterity, jumping power and special abilities. With nothing but their paws, ears and a lot of attitude, these fluffy bunnies turn into tough guys as soon as they get into the ring.

These rabbits originally did martial arts because it was cool. However martial arts is practised for a variety of reasons, including self-defence, competition, physical health and fitness. Showing amazing dedication and skill for ones so young, these 'pocket rockets' displayed their skills with loud support and applause from every corner of the grandstand.

I know lots of people who practise martial arts. They would all love to receive figurines like these! If you use the same basic ideas, you can turn virtually all of the figurine characters in this book into ninjas.

EQUIPMENT
Small kitchen knife
Medium paintbrush
Zip-lock bag
Frilling tool
Small rolling pin

MATERIALS – 1 RABBIT
Tylose
20 g (¾ oz) white icing (body)
1 pea-sized ball of black or other coloured icing (belt)
2 x 6 g (⅛ oz) white icing (legs and arms)
4 pea-sized balls of grey icing (paws)
50 g (1¾ oz) grey icing (head)
Dried spaghetti
1 grape-sized ball of grey icing (ears)
2 pea-sized balls of pink icing (ears)

1 pea-sized ball of black icing (eyes)

2 pea-sized balls of grey icing (whisker cheeks)

1 pea-sized ball of pink icing (nose)

1 pea-sized ball of white icing (teeth)

COLOUR THE FONDANT ICING

Mix the colours the day before if possible, to make intense colours easier to work with. For instructions on how to colour fondant icing, see pages 178–179.

MEASURE AND ROLL

Measure each amount of icing required per body part, then roll each into a ball. Place in a zip-lock bag so they don't dry out.

BODY

Roll your 20 g (¾ oz) ball of white icing into a cone. Place the wide end down on a flat work surface.

Mark a line where the belt is to be placed, then mark the chest with a 'Y' for the jacket (photo 1).

BELT

Roll your pea-sized ball of black icing into a thin sausage. Trim it at each end with your knife, then wrap it around your rabbit's waist where you made the belt imprint, securing it with a dab of water.

LEGS AND ARMS

Roll your two 6 g (⅛ oz) balls of white icing, making sure they are soft and crack-free. Roll each one into a fat sausage, which is flat at each end. One sausage will become the arms, the other the legs.

Using a sharp knife, cut the sausages on an angle in the middle (photo 2). Soften at the joints (the angle), then stick the arms and legs onto your rabbit with a dab of water.

PAWS

Shape your four pea-sized balls of grey icing into teardrop shapes, by gently rolling one side thinner.

Flatten the teardrops with your finger to make a paw. Using the back of a knife, make indentations

7

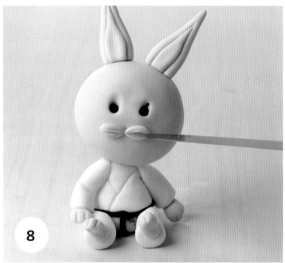

8

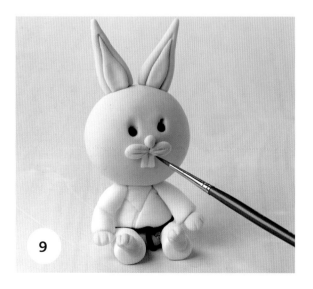

9

on the top of the paws for the toes (photo 3, page 147) — or you may want to make a karate-chop paw!

Stick the paws on the end of the rabbit's arms and legs with a dab of water. Pinch the paws into place with your fingers.

HEAD

Roll your 50 g (1¾ oz) ball of grey icing, making sure it is soft, crack-free and a perfect round shape.

Place the ball in the palm of your dry, clean hand. Now place your other hand over the top as though you are about to clap. Gently and evenly press down on the ball with both hands, to make it flatter (photo 4, page 147).

Insert one 5 cm (2 in) length of dried spaghetti halfway into the base of the head. Secure the head onto the body, by inserting the exposed end of spaghetti into the body (photo 5, page 147).

EARS

Roll your grape-sized ball of grey icing into a cylinder shape, then cut it in half crossways. Take each half and roll each into a 4 cm (1½ in) cylinder. Flatten slightly and indent with the frilling tool (photo 6, page 147).

Roll your two pea-sized balls of pink icing into a cone shape, slightly smaller than the grey ears. Stick them in the indentation on the grey ears with a dab of water.

Attach the ears to the head with 3 cm (1¼ in) lengths of dried spaghetti.

EYES

Using your frilling tool or the end of a paintbrush, poke two small holes in the head for the eyes (photo 7).

Roll two small balls from the pea-sized ball of black icing and stick them in the holes to form the pupils.

WHISKER CHEEKS

Gently squash your two pea-sized balls of grey icing between your fingers to make the whisker cheeks you want. Stick them onto the front of the face with a dab of water.

WHISKERS

Using the back of your knife, make three whisker lines on each side of your rabbit's whisker cheeks (photo 8).

NOSE

Roll your pea-sized ball of pink icing and pinch it slightly to form a little triangle (just like a rabbit's nose). Stick the nose just on top of the middle of the whisker cheeks with a dab of water.

TEETH

Roll your pea-sized ball of white icing out to 2 mm ($\frac{1}{16}$ in) thick. Using a knife, cut it into a square, then mark a line on the front of your square to create two big rabbit teeth.

Stick the teeth onto your rabbit's face, just below, and in between, its whisker cheeks, with a dab of water (photo 9).

SPORTY DOGS

Sporty dogs are for anyone who loves sport. These figurines are definitely not for people like me who cannot swim, catch a ball or run around the block without gasping for breath. These figurines are for people who are incredibly, well, sporty!

Sporty dogs spend their mornings exercising; their houses are usually full of workout equipment and they pride themselves on their fitness. Throughout the seasons, sporty dogs are playing all sorts of sports and perform all sorts of important jobs, like being rescue dogs or police dogs.

These are great cake toppers for anyone you know who is sports mad. So if you are making a sporty figurine for yourself or someone else, think about a favourite sport — or maybe you have a favourite sporting hero?

You can make these toppers extra special by making a ball based on their favourite sport — for example a football or baseball — and you can even include the colours of their favourite sports team, either with the figurine or on the base cake.

EQUIPMENT
Small kitchen knife
Medium paintbrush
Zip-lock bag
Frilling tool

MATERIALS – 1 SPORTY DOG
Tylose
20 g (¾ oz) coloured icing (body)
2 pea-sized balls of coloured icing (back legs)
1 grape-sized ball of coloured icing (front legs)
50 g (1¾ oz) coloured icing (head)
Dried spaghetti
2 pea-sized balls of coloured icing (ears)
1 pea-sized ball of black icing (eyes)
1 peanut-sized ball of coloured icing (tail)
1 pea-sized ball of black icing (nose)

COLOUR THE FONDANT ICING

Mix the colours the day before if possible, to make intense colours easier to work with. For instructions on how to colour fondant icing, see pages 178–179.

MEASURE AND ROLL

Measure each amount of icing required per body part, then roll each into a ball. Place in a zip-lock bag so they don't dry out.

BODY

Roll your 20 g (¾ oz) ball of coloured icing into a pear shape. Lay it out flat (photo 1).

BACK LEGS

Roll your two pea-sized balls of coloured icing into teardrop shapes by gently rolling one side thinner. Flatten the teardrops with your finger, then indent them with the back of a knife on the wide ends to make paws.

Stick the paws underneath the body with a dab of water. Pinch the paws into place with your fingers.

FRONT LEGS

Roll your grape-sized ball of coloured icing into a sausage. Using a knife, cut the sausage on an angle in the middle. Roll one end of each sausage slightly thinner than the other. On the wide end, indent two paw marks using the back of the knife.

Stick the front legs onto your dog with a dab of water (photo 2). For a bended leg, use the back of a knife and indent the joint before sticking the front legs onto the body.

HEAD

Roll your 50 g (1¾ oz) ball of coloured icing, making sure it is soft, crack-free and a perfect round shape. Place it on a flat surface. Using your index finger, gently press on one side of the ball to flatten it slightly, to give you a puppy's head shape.

Using the back of a sharp knife, mark the mouth by cutting an upside down 'V' shape below the nose (photo 3).

Insert two 3 cm (1¼ in) lengths of spaghetti halfway into the base of the head. Secure the head onto the body, by inserting the exposed ends of spaghetti into the body.

EARS

Roll the other two pea-sized balls of coloured icing into oval-shape puppy ears using your fingers (photo 4). Stick the ears onto the top of the head with a dab of water (photo 5).

EYES

Using your frilling tool or the end of a paintbrush, poke two small holes in the head for the eyes. Roll two small balls from the pea-sized ball of black icing and place them in the holes.

TAIL

Roll your peanut-sized ball of coloured icing into a long sausage. Flatten one end with your finger, then stick that end under the body with a dab of water. For a curled tail, wrap the tail around your little finger or a pencil or paintbrush, then gently let it go, keeping some of the curl.

NOSE

Squash your remaining pea-sized ball of black icing between your fingers to make the nose shape you want — it looks better when it's slightly oval. Stick it onto the front of your puppy's face with a dab of water (photo 6).

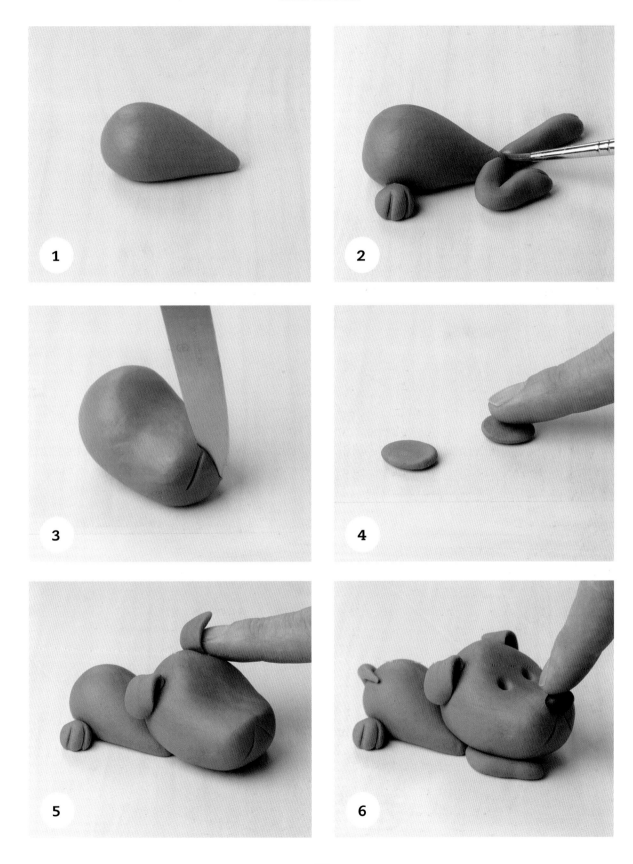

ANGEL BABIES

A new little baby has been born into our family. Her name is Tilly, and everyone has gone absolutely crazy. My mother and auntie stare at her while she is sleeping, and are quite convinced she is the most beautiful baby they have ever seen, although my mother told me I was also a beautiful baby, which was some comfort.

Everyone has raced around buying Tilly presents. She has more toys than anyone I know, and she is not even old enough to play with them. Her parents photograph her every move, and when she needs a nappy change my family thinks it's really cute.

So why is there so much crazy fuss around this little baby? Because she is the newest member of our family. We love to guess who she looks like the most (she has blonde hair like me). Most importantly, we want her to feel as loved as possible, so that she will always feel confident and happy. That's what makes a baby so special.

Let's face it, they are also pretty darn cute, and if you have a baby brother, sister or cousin, I can promise you that you will probably be their biggest hero. So what better cake for a baby or someone who is having a baby than a baby figurine?

You can personalise this figurine even more with its hair colour (or no hair), outfits, dimples, or just the baby's expression — especially if it is a grizzly baby who cries a lot!

EQUIPMENT
Small kitchen knife
Medium paintbrush
Zip-lock bag
Frilling tool

MATERIALS – 1 ANGEL BABY
Tylose
20 g ($^3/_4$ oz) coloured icing (body)
20 g ($^3/_4$ oz) coloured icing (legs)
6 g ($^1/_8$ oz) coloured icing (arms)
4 pea-sized balls of skin-coloured icing (hands and feet)
50 g ($1^3/_4$ oz) skin-coloured icing (head)
Dried spaghetti
2 pea-sized balls of skin-coloured icing (ears)
1 pea-sized ball of black icing (eyes)
2 pea-sized balls of white icing (wings)
Red petal dust (cheeks; optional)
Cornflour (cornstarch) (cheeks; optional)

COLOUR THE FONDANT ICING

Mix the colours the day before if possible, to make intense colours easier to work with. For instructions on how to colour fondant icing, see pages 178–179.

MEASURE AND ROLL

Measure each amount of icing required per body part, then roll each into a ball. Place in a zip-lock bag so they don't dry out.

BODY

Roll your 20 g (¾ oz) ball of coloured icing into a pear shape. Sit the wide end down.

LEGS

Roll your other 20 g (¾ oz) ball of coloured icing into a cylinder. Using a knife, cut the cylinder on an angle in the middle (photo 1). Soften at the hip joint (the angle), then stick the legs onto your baby with a dab of water.

ARMS

Roll your 6 g (⅛ oz) ball of coloured icing into a cylinder. Using a knife, cut it on an angle in the middle (photo 2). Soften at the shoulder joint (the angle), then stick the arms onto your baby with a dab of water.

BUTTONS

Using a frilling tool or the end of a piping nozzle, indent buttons up the front of the body to make a jumpsuit (photo 3).

HANDS AND FEET

Roll your four balls of skin-coloured icing into teardrop shapes. Using the back of a knife, mark lines for the toes on two teardrop shapes. On the other two, cut a thumb for the hands, and mark three lines for fingers. Attach them with a dab of water (photo 4).

HEAD

Roll your 50 g (1¾ oz) ball of skin-coloured icing, making sure it is soft, crack-free and a perfect round shape. Place the ball in the palm of your dry, clean hand.

Now place your other hand over the top as though you are about to clap. Gently and evenly press down on the ball with both hands, to make it flatter (photo 5).

Insert two 3 cm (1¼ in) lengths of dried spaghetti halfway into the top of the body to support the head. Stick the head on.

EARS

Roll your two pea-sized balls of skin-coloured icing into tiny balls. Stick them to the sides of the head with a dab of water. Using your frilling tool, make an indent in each ear (photo 6).

EYES

Using a frilling tool or the end of a paintbrush, poke two small holes in the head for the eyes. Roll two small balls from the black icing and place them in the holes.

MOUTH

Using the end of your paintbrush, poke a small mouth hole onto the baby's face.

WINGS

Roll your two pea-sized balls of white icing into teardrop shapes, then flatten them. Stick them onto the baby's back with water, then shape into wings with your fingers.

CHEEKS (OPTIONAL)

To create the sweetest rosy cheeks, dilute some red petal dust with cornflour and dust it on with a dry paintbrush. (Test it on a spare bit of skin-coloured icing first.)

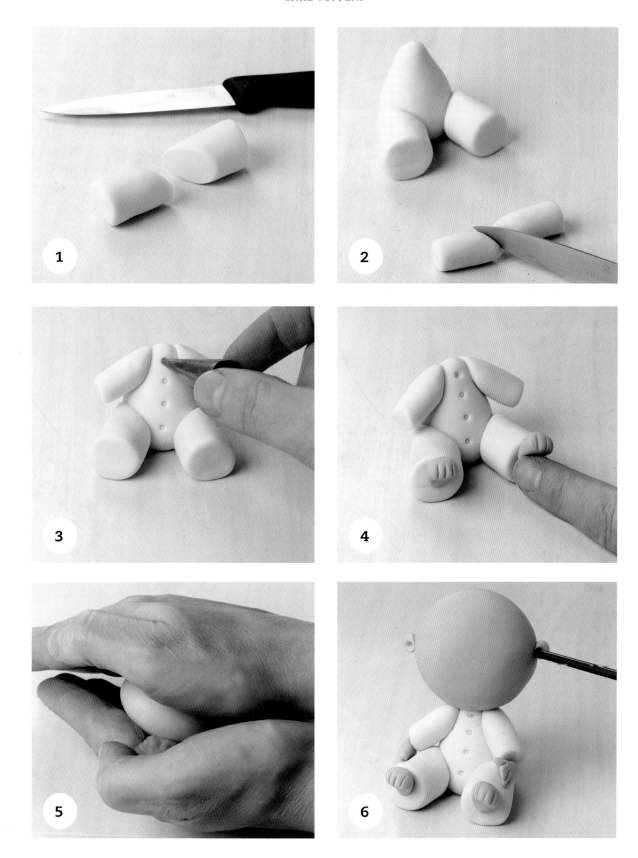

SUPERHERO FAMILY

I have a really wonderful family full of crazy people. The oldest family member is 96, the youngest is a baby, and then there's everyone in between. My brother is really stinky and never cleans up after himself; my Dad is everyone's favourite; I have a stepmother whose laugh is so loud she nearly blows your ear drums out, and my Mum loves gardening. Then there is my daughter, Estelle, who is horse crazy. And as for me … I'm the 'princess' in the family, so everyone likes to tease me.

Everyone's family is different, and that's the most wonderful thing about them. So when you are making your family figurines, don't think about just the people you live with, but anyone you love and consider to be a really important person.

The figurines work best when you think about what makes that person unique in your family. When I make a figurine of my brother, I always have him surrounded by old pizza boxes and dead apple cores, because he is such a grub. If I was to make a figurine of my Mum, she would be holding a flower.

Maybe there is someone in your family who is extra special? Every family has a superhero — or maybe two! So why don't you give this person a superhero cape for their figurine? How cool is that! And remember you can make their outfit in their favourite colours.

I think I will give a superhero cape to my Dad's figurine — he is my hero!

EQUIPMENT
Small kitchen knife
Medium paintbrush
Zip-lock bag
Frilling tool
Rolling pin
Clay gun (optional)
Large plastic straw

MATERIALS – 1 ADULT
Tylose
30 g (1 oz) skin-coloured icing (head)
40 g (1½ oz) coloured icing (body)
5 g (⅛ oz) contrasting coloured icing (undies)
5 g (⅛ oz) black icing (shoes)
Dried spaghetti
2 grape-sized balls of coloured icing (same as body, for arms)
1 peanut-sized ball of skin-coloured icing (hands)
15 g (½ oz) coloured icing (cape; optional)
1 pea-sized ball of white icing (eyes)
1 pea-sized ball of black icing (eyes)
2 pea-sized balls of skin-coloured icing (ears)
20 g (¾ oz) coloured icing (hair)

MATERIALS – 1 KID

15 g (½ oz) skin-coloured icing (head)

20 g (¾ oz) coloured icing (body)

1 grape-sized ball of contrasting coloured icing (undies)

1 grape-sized ball of black icing (shoes)

Dried spaghetti

2 peanut-sized balls of coloured icing (same as body, for arms)

1 pea-sized ball of skin-coloured icing (hands)

10 g (¼ oz) coloured icing (cape; optional)

1 pea-sized ball white icing (eyes)

1 pea-sized ball black icing (eyes)

1 pea-sized ball of skin-coloured icing (ears), cut in half

10 g (¼ oz) coloured icing (hair)

MATERIALS – 1 BABY

15 g (½ oz) skin-coloured icing (head)

10 g (¼ oz) coloured icing (body)

1 grape-sized ball of contrasting coloured icing (undies)

2 pea-sized balls of coloured icing (same as body, for legs)

1 pea-sized ball of contrasting coloured icing (feet)

2 pea-sized balls of skin-coloured icing (arms)

5 g (⅛ oz) coloured icing (cape; optional)

2 pea-sized balls of contrasting coloured icings (dummy)

1 pea-sized ball of skin-coloured icing (ears)

Dried spaghetti

1 grape-sized ball of coloured icing (hair quiff)

SUPERHERO ADULT

Colour the fondant icing: Mix the colours the day before if possible, to make intense colours easier to work with. For instructions on how to colour fondant icing, see pages 178–179.

Measure and roll: Measure each amount of icing required per body part, then roll each into a ball. Place in a zip-lock bag so they don't dry out.

Head: Roll your 30 g (1 oz) ball of skin-coloured icing, making sure it is soft, crack-free and a perfect round shape.

Body: Roll your 40 g (1½ oz) ball of coloured icing into a cylinder shape, 6 cm (2½ in) long. Cut in half with a knife (photo 1).

Undies: Flatten your 5 g (⅛ oz) ball of contrasting coloured icing into a disc, the same circumference as the body. Pinch down the front, to make the undies shape (photo 2).

Shoes: Squash your 5 g (⅛ oz) ball of black icing into a disc, the same circumference as the body (photo 3).

Assemble the body: Stick the undies between the upper and lower body parts, with a dab of water. Stick the shoes (black disc) on the bottom of the body with a dab of water. Gently roll the cylinder so all the bits meld together (photo 4).

To make the legs, use the back of a knife to indent a line down the middle of the bottom half of the body, from the undies to the shoes (photo 5).

Insert two 3 cm (1¼ in) lengths of dried spaghetti halfway in the neck of the body. Lie the body flat on a work surface and allow to dry.

Arms and hands: Roll your two grape-sized balls of coloured icing into sausages, then stick them onto

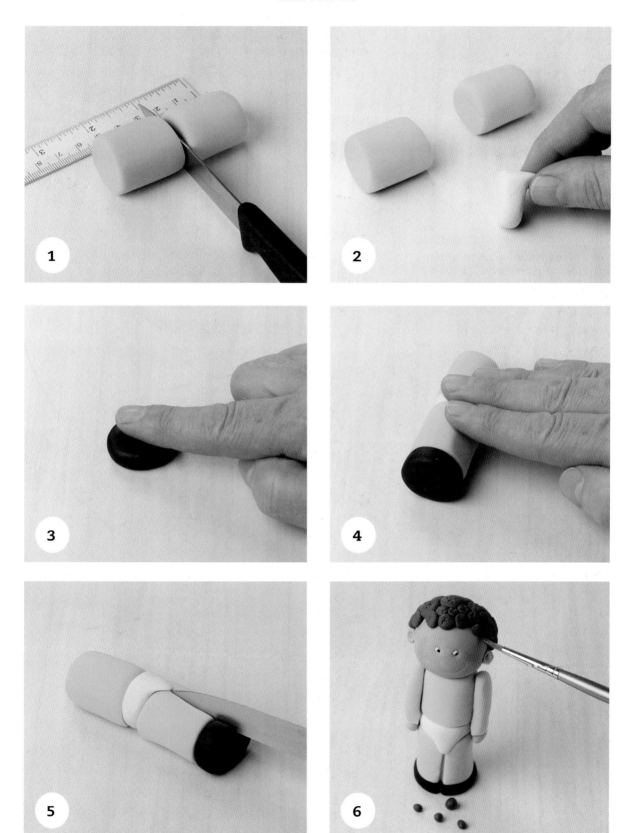

the sides of the body with a dab of water, keeping the arms flat to the sides.

To make the hands, split your peanut-sized ball of skin-coloured icing into two pieces. Roll each into a ball, then stick them onto the end of your arms. Use the back of a knife to mark the fingers.

Cape (optional): Roll your 15 g (½ oz) ball of coloured icing out to 3 mm (⅛ in) thick. Using a knife, cut a rectangle 6 cm (2½ in) wide, and about the same height of your superhero. Stick the cape onto its shoulders, curling back about the top 1 cm (½ in) of the cape to create a collar.

Face: Using your frilling tool or the end of a paintbrush, poke two small holes in the head for the eyes. Roll two small balls from the white icing and place them in the holes. Roll two smaller balls of black icing and place them on top as the pupils. Indent the mouth with a plastic straw or the back of a knife. Attach the head to the body, on the spaghetti.

Ears: Roll your two pea-sized balls of skin-coloured icing into tiny balls. Stick them to the sides of the head with a dab of water. Using your frilling tool, make an indent in each ear.

Hair
Curly hair: Take your 20 g (¾ oz) ball of coloured icing and knead it until it is smooth and pliable. Pinch small pieces off, roll into tiny balls, then stick onto the head with dabs of water (photo 6, page 161).

Cool dude hair: Knead your 20 g (¾ oz) ball of coloured icing auntil it is smooth and pliable. Roll out to 2 mm (¹⁄₁₆ in) thick.

Cut out small, elongated triangles, then stick the pointy ends onto the head with a dab of water. Roll the rest of the hair up.

Mum's hair: Take your 20 g (¾ oz) ball of coloured icing and knead it until it is smooth and pliable. Roll out to 2 mm (¹⁄₁₆ in) thick. Press through a clay gun to form spaghetti strands, then glue onto the head with a dab of water.

Grandma hair: Take your 20 g (¾ oz) ball of coloured icing and knead it until it is smooth and pliable. Roll out to 2 mm (¹⁄₁₆ in) thick. Using a knife, cut out a circle and stick it on top of the head; cut the excess off with scissors. Make a small ball with the excess icing and stick it on top with a dab of water to create a bun. Using the back of a knife, create the hair lines.

SUPERHERO KID
Follow the directions for the Superhero adult. Remember that all the body parts will be smaller.

SUPER HERO BABY
Colour, measure and roll the icing, the same as for the Superhero adult.

Head: Roll your 15 g (½ oz) ball of skin-coloured icing, making sure it is soft, crack-free and a perfect round shape (photo 1).

Body and undies: For the body, roll your 10 g (¼ oz) ball of coloured icing into a pear shape. For the undies, squash your grape-sized ball of coloured icing into a disc the same size as the bottom of the body — you may need to trim it with a knife. Stick the disc on the bottom of the body with a dab

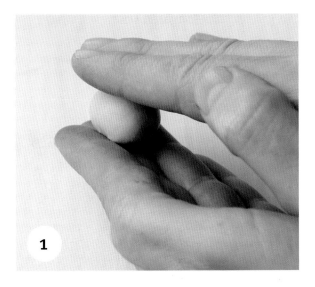

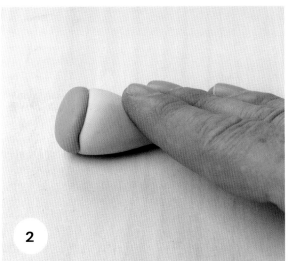

of water, then roll the body around to 'meld' the disc to the bottom of the body (photo 2).

Legs and feet: For the legs, roll your two pea-sized balls of coloured icing into two sausages. Soften at the hip joint (the angle), then attach to the baby with a dab of water.

For the feet, split your other pea-sized ball of coloured icing in half and roll into two balls. Squash the balls into two discs, the same size as the end of the legs. Stick onto the legs with a dab of water.

Arms: Roll your two pea-sized balls of skin-coloured icing into sausages. Stick them onto the body with a dab of water. Rest them on the legs if you like.

Cape (optional): Same as for the adult, using your 5 g (⅛ oz) ball of coloured icing.

Face and dummy: Using the plastic straw, indent two eyelids for the baby, or make the eyes the same as the adult using small balls of white and black icing.

To make the dummy, take your two pea-sized balls of contrasting coloured icing — two different colours work best — and make sure one ball is half the size of the other. Squash them flat and stick them onto the baby's mouth with a dab of water.

To make the ears, roll your pea-sized ball of skin-coloured icing into two tiny balls. Stick them to the head with a dab of water.

Attach the head to the body using a 5 cm (2 in) length of dried spaghetti

Hair quiff: Roll your grape-sized ball of coloured icing into a small cone. Twist the cone and attach it to the head with a dab of water (photo 3).

TRICKS OF THE TRADE

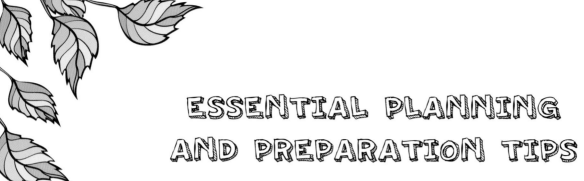

ESSENTIAL PLANNING AND PREPARATION TIPS

PLANNING

Two weeks before making your cake, check through the recipe to ensure you have all the materials and ingredients required. Making and decorating cakes always takes longer than you think, and being well organised makes for a more enjoyable experience.

Remember that some specialist products or equipment might not always be in stock and may need to be ordered in advance from a supplier.

DESIGNING

The designs in this book can be followed to the letter or, as you gain more confidence, tailored to your own needs.

The easiest thing to change is the colour palette, but you can also change the decoration details. The techniques are also easily adapted, once you have learned them. And of course you can interchange the cake toppers and cake designs.

Note: Remember that some cake toppers use non-edible elements such as toothpicks that must be removed before the cake is served.

PREPARING THE WORK SPACE

I cannot emphasise enough how vital it is to prepare your work space before you start.

Make sure you have everything you require, including: room in the freezer if you're going to freeze your cake before decorating; adequate bench space and boards; all the equipment and ingredients to hand, such as cornflour (cornstarch) for lightly dusting your work surface and plastic sheets.

RTR icing dries out very quickly, so always wrap unused icing in plastic. If it is already rolled out, cover it with a plastic sheet.

THE THREE-DAY RULE

The three-day rule is very important. If you really want to create a wonderful, professional-looking cake, this is the time that it will require, and it is futile — and stressful — to try to hurry it.

Cakes that are not given time to cool, or ganache that has not been allowed to set properly, will make poor foundations for the rest of the decoration.

Day 1: Bake your cake and allow adequate cooling time. Most of our cakes (pages 24–27) can be kept for up to a week in an airtight container in the fridge, or in the freezer for 2 months before decorating.

Day 2: Cut and ganache the cake (see Cake techniques, pages 28–41) and allow adequate setting time.

Day 3: Decorate the cake.

Here are some more tips for giving your cakes that professional look.

GANACHE

Have a good look at how we set up our cakes with ganache to achieve very clean and sharp edges. Ganache also tastes much better than the buttercream that some people use, and another advantage is that it keeps the cake fresh for much longer.

RTR ICING

At Planet Cake we only use ready-to-roll (RTR) fondant icing, which finishes with a nice satin shine and is very reliable. We always buy this ready made, but if you want to make your own, see the recipe on page 175.

We set up our cakes by first covering them with a smooth layer of ganache that sets hard and hides any imperfections, giving a perfect foundation. This allows us to use only a thin layer of RTR icing.

USING A PASTA MACHINE

One of our 'tricks' at Planet Cake is to use a pasta machine to evenly roll out icing. If you don't already own a pasta machine, buy a cheap one and you'll find it much easier than using a traditional rolling pin.

You can even use the spaghetti-making setting to make hair for the Superhero family (as seen in the photo on page 158).

USING A FLEXI-SCRAPER

Another useful item is our flexi-scraper — one of our proudest inventions! You can make one yourself out of stiff plastic, so that it is firm but remains flexible (see Glossary entry on page 171).

We use the flexi-scraper for buffing and polishing the icing, which is the 'secret' to the sharp edges that give our cakes their professional look.

STORING AND TRANSPORTING YOUR CAKE

Keep your decorated cake away from water, as water will 'burn' the icing and leave it stained. Sunlight will fade the colour of the icing and heat will soften it, so decorations may melt or droop.

However, never put the iced cake in the fridge, as the damp environment will make the icing 'sweat'.

Store the finished cake in a cake box, putting a non-slip rubber mat under the cake board to stop the cake moving.

TOOLS OF THE TRADE

This is the basic set of equipment you will need to make figurines and decorate cakes. You don't need to buy all these tools at once — you might prefer to start with some simple items, such as a set of circle cutters, icing smoothers and a palette knife, and then slowly build up your tool box.

1 Styrofoam egg (for Baby dragons)
2 Frilling tool
3 Balling tool
4 Broad and fine paintbrushes; 2B pencil
5 Non-slip rubber mat
6 Alphabet cutters (for birthday messages)
7 Ruler, to measure
8 Zip-lock bags, to store icing
9 Tape measure
10 Scissors, to snip fondant for decorations
11 Dried spaghetti, to support figurine parts
12 Styrofoam block to store cake toppers (optional)
13 Comb scraper (optional)
14 Flexi-scraper (round-cornered piece of acetate), to smooth icing
15 Clay gun (optional)
16 Plain piping nozzle (Graveyard cake)
17 Star piping nozzle (Cartoon cake)
18 Sharp kitchen knife
19 Dropper
20 Stitching tool (Martial arts ring cake)
21 Toothpicks
22 Circle cutters
23 Large plastic straw
24 Small rolling pin
25 A4 paper and baking paper, to make templates

GLOSSARY

Many items listed here are available from specialist cake-decorating stores. Some of the more everyday bits can be bought at the supermarket or cookware shops.

Acetate film is often described as plastic film or sheeting. This general-purpose plastic is an industry standard in graphic arts, packaging, printing and for overlays.

Alphabet cutters are great for cake decorators and chefs. You can buy them as a set in either tin or plastic, and different fonts are usually available.

Balling tool This long plastic stick has a ball at either end. Use it to make round indentations and smooth curves in modelling or to shape flower petals.

Cake boards are usually made from silver or gold masonite and are available from cake-decorating supply shops.

Set-up or temp cake boards are the same size as the cake — for example, a 22 cm (9 in) round cake on a 22 cm (9 in) round board — and they operate as a guide for ganaching and a way to easily handle the cake and not stain the display board.

The display cake board or 'final' board is the larger board the cake is placed on as part of its display; the display board is 10–15 cm (4–6 in) larger than the cake.

Clay gun We use a clay gun in place of a sugar-craft gun. You can use either, but we find the clay gun cheaper and sturdier. It is available from hobby shops.

Comb scraper is great for marking and embossing a serrated pattern. It has lots of different sugar-craft uses, and is made in either plastic or stainless steel. Its most common shape is a triangle or rectangle, but it comes in other shapes as well. It is available from cake-decorating stores.

Cornflour (cornstarch) is used in cake decorating for dusting the work surface when rolling out icing. It must be used sparingly, as it can dry the icing out, but it is finer to use than icing sugar.

Couverture is a natural, sweet chocolate containing no added fats other than natural cocoa butter. It is used for dipping, moulding, coating and similar purposes.

Cutters are available in different sizes and shapes and often come in sets, in plastic or stainless steel.

Decorating alcohol has 5% rose essence and is used for painting and removing icing stains. Vodka can be used as a substitute.

Disposable plastic piping bags are available in most cake-decorating stores and some supermarkets.

Edible glitter is sold in an array of colours, and usually applied with water or piping gel.

Flexi-scraper is a Planet Cake DIY invention. We use either unused X-ray film (which can be hard to get), or a thin plastic, such as acetate, computer film or the plastic used for flexible display folders (the ones with the plastic sleeves inside).

Cut the plastic to a rectangle, a little larger than the palm of your hand. Round the edges using scissors, then disinfect the plastic and hey presto!

Use the flexi-scraper to buff and polish the icing, helping you create razor-sharp edges and very smooth surfaces. The flexi-scraper is flexible, so you can manipulate it with your hand to navigate the icing of shaped and complex cakes, to eliminate all the air bubbles and bumps in the icing, resulting in a smooth, perfect and professional-looking icing finish.

Florist's tape can be twisted on its own to create an effect, but it can also be used to cover wires or dowels before inserting them into the cake. Some are coated with a green paper.

Florist's wire is available from cake-decorating stores. It is used to add support to three-dimensional icing elements and for helping to attach them to the cake. It comes in several different thicknesses (called gauges). We mostly use 22-gauge wire.

When making cakes for children, it is better to use dried spaghetti.

Food colour Paste colouring is the most concentrated of food colours. Mix this paste directly into your fondant icing to colour it, or mix it with alcohol to paint with. Liquid colouring is similar but less intense.

Frilling tool is used to 'frill' soft surfaces, such as sugar paste, modelling paste, flower paste or marzipan.

Ganache is a mixture of chocolate and cream. It can be made with dark, milk or white chocolate and is used as a filling or icing for cakes.

Gel/piping gel is a clear, sticky gel that becomes fluid when warmed. It maintains a shiny wet look when set. It is also known as piping jelly.

Glaze is a product or mixture that gives a shiny appearance to cakes or decorations.

'Glue' To fix decorations or sections of icing to the top of cupcakes, simply add a dab of water. Use this 'adhesive' to attach the components as you would use glue, taking care not to get things too wet.

Glycerine is a colourless, odourless, syrupy liquid made from fats and oils, and used to retain moisture and add sweetness to foods. Stir into icing to restore consistency, or use it to soften fondant icing or royal icing. It can also be used to soften dried icing colours.

Marzipan or almond paste is made from ground blanched almonds and icing sugar. It is used as a very thin layer on fruitcakes before they are covered with royal icing or sugar paste. Marzipan can also be used for making flowers and fruit.

Non-slip rubber mats are perfect for placing under your turntable or cake to prevent slipping. A mat is also great underneath the cake when placing it in a cake box for transport.

Paintbrushes Fine paintbrushes can be used for painting, brushing crumbs or icing (confectioners') sugar out of tricky corners, as well as applying powdered or liquid colours. Broad brushes are useful for cleaning debris off the cake board.

Painting Mix edible colour paste or liquid colour with decorating alcohol, then paint onto fondant-covered cakes with a fine paintbrush.

Palette knife A flat metal knife used to smooth ganache, and also handy for transferring the cake from a set-up board to the display board. There is also a 'cranked' palette knife, which has a bend (crank) in the blade, and usually a plastic handle. It is used to spread and smooth ganache onto cakes and cupcakes. Both types come in large and small sizes.

Pasta machine is also called a pasta maker. Used for making home-made pasta, it is also useful for rolling out icing as it provides a consistent thickness and rolls the icing perfectly.

Piping tips and coupler These are specially shaped, open-end tips used to form icing decorations. The size and shape of the opening on a piping tip determines the type of decorations the tip will produce. Round piping tips are used to make dots and outlines, as well as for writing and figure piping.

The coupler sits between a material piping bag and piping tip. You can then screw the piping tip onto the coupler and easily change between different sizes and shapes without changing the piping bag.

90° plastic scraper is simply a scraper (see next page), held on a 90° angle.

Powders and dusts are available in petal, pearl, sparkle and lustre finishes. Some decorators mix the powder with decorating alcohol and apply the colour directly. The lustre and pearl powders create a luminous effect to sugar flowers.

Pre-coloured icing To make red or black icing, you will need pre-coloured icing, which is available from cake-decorating supply stores. The advantage of pre-coloured icing is the intensity of the colour pigment.

Rolled fondant icing Also called RTR (ready-to-roll), plastic icing, sugar paste and fondant, this is a dough-like icing that is rolled out, draped over the cake and then smoothed down. It is used to cover cakes and cupcakes. The basic ingredient is icing (confectioners') sugar, with the addition of gelatine, corn syrup (or glucose) and glycerine to make a malleable sweet paste.

Fondant gives the cake a beautiful, porcelain-like surface that can be painted, piped, quilted, cut out or stamped. Fondant comes in white or ivory and can be tinted to any colour of the rainbow.

It is also used to model and cut three-dimensional shapes for decoration, such as ribbons, bows and cut-outs. Good-quality fondant is costly but worth buying.

Rolling pins A small rolling pin is ideal for small projects and rolling out small pieces of icing. You can buy a fancy one from a cake-decorating supply store, but the most prized small rolling pins at Planet Cake are those found in children's baking sets.

We also use large rolling pins to roll out icing. The types available are: without handles; with integral handles; or, our favourite, with handles that are attached to a central rod in the roller.

Rolling pins, whether made from wood, marble or silicone, should have absolutely smooth surfaces, with no dints or marks that will transfer to your icing.

Royal icing is a mixture of egg white (or albumen) and icing sugar, with a little lemon juice or vinegar. It can be coloured with edible food colour and spread over cakes and boards, and sets very hard. It is also used for piping.

You can buy instant royal icing mixes where you just have to add water, or you can make your own using the recipe on page 177.

Scraper Best made of stainless steel, a scraper is a flat piece of metal or plastic with a straight side that is used for scraping the excess ganache off the side of a cake when you are preparing and filling it. Metal scrapers can be sourced from cake-decorating stores and the internet. If you don't have a scraper you can use a metal ruler. Plastic scrapers are also fine to use.

Smoothers are also called 'paddles'. These rectangular, flat plastic paddles with handles are used for pressing the air bubbles out of fondant icing and rubbing it to a smooth shiny finish. For covering cakes, you always need at least two smoothers.

Stitching tool, more properly known as a tracing wheel, is an instrument with serrated teeth on a wheel attached to a handle. A stitching tool is used in sewing to transfer markings from patterns onto fabric, but this tool also makes a perfect stitching effect in RTR icing.

There are two basic types of tracing wheels: one with a serrated edge, and one with a smooth edge. You need to buy the serrated-edged tracing wheel, available from haberdashers.

Styrofoam egg is a styrofoam ball in the shape of an egg; they can also be called styrofoam Easter eggs and styrofoam balls. Available from craft and hobby stores.

Syrup, sugar syrup or soaking syrup is a mixture made from equal amounts of boiled water and jam (see recipe page 176). The syrup is brushed over the cut surfaces of cakes to prevent them drying out before icing, or between the ganache and icing covering to help adhere the icing. Syrup can be flavoured with alcohol such as Cointreau.

Turntable is a useful tool when you are coating cakes with royal icing or rolled fondant (RTR) icing, as it lets you approach the cake from all sides. You can buy a turntable from a cake-decorating store, but at Planet Cake we actually like to use the type that you would put under a TV set!

Tylose powder can be mixed into rolled fondant, marzipan or royal icing and forms a strong modelling paste that dries hard. Tylose powder can also be mixed with a small amount of water to make thick and strong edible glue.

ICING RECIPES

Ganache

The ideal chocolate for ganache is a couverture variety, with a cocoa content of 53–63 per cent. In cold weather you might have to add a little more cream or reduce the chocolate a bit so your ganache isn't too hard. If you can't find couverture, try dark chocolate from the supermarket confectionery section.

Preparation: 15 minutes
Cooking: 10 minutes
Makes about 1.8 kg (4 lb), enough to cover each cake in this book (with some left over in case of mishaps)

White ganache

1.3 kg (3 lb) white chocolate, finely chopped
450 ml (16 fl oz) pure cream

Dark ganache

1.2 kg (2 lb 10 oz) dark chocolate, finely chopped
600 ml (21 fl oz) pure cream

1 Put the white or dark chocolate pieces in a large bowl.
2 Pour the cream into a saucepan and bring to boiling point. Pour the cream over the chocolate and mix with a hand whisk until the ganache is smooth. (Don't use electric beaters, as you will create too many air bubbles in the ganache.)
3 Allow to cool completely, then leave to set overnight.

MICROWAVE METHOD

1 Put the chocolate and cream in a microwave-proof bowl. Heat on high for 1–2 minutes, then remove and stir. Keep heating and then stirring until the ganache is smooth.
2 Remove the bowl from the microwave, cover with plastic wrap and leave for 5 minutes. Shake the bowl a little so all the chocolate sinks to the bottom.
3 Mix with a hand whisk until smooth.
4 Allow to cool completely, then leave to set overnight.

GANACHE TIPS

- We use either white or dark chocolate ganache under the fondant icing on all our cakes. We use white ganache with vanilla and citrus-flavoured cakes, but please note that in hot weather, white ganache is less stable than dark ganache and won't set as firmly.
- Avoid using dark chocolate with a cocoa content of more than 63 per cent. It is more likely to burn when heated, and separates easily. It may also be too bitter in contrast to the sweet fondant icing, and will set very hard, as it contains very little cocoa butter.
- We use pure cream (single cream), not thickened or thick (double) cream. A cream with a lower fat content (but not low-fat) is best as it won't thicken when mixed.
- Ganache will keep for about 1 week in an airtight container in the fridge, so check the

174

use-by date of the cream you are using. Ganache also freezes well. If you make a large batch, freeze it in small containers so you can thaw just the quantity needed.

- Always bring ganache to room temperature before using.
- If your ganache needs reheating to soften it slightly, place the amount you need in a microwave-proof dish and heat it in 10-second bursts on medium power (50%), stirring between each burst, until it reaches the desired consistency.

Fondant icing

At Planet Cake, we don't make our own fondant icing, as we find the commercial varieties convenient and often more reliable to use. If you do need a recipe, this one is courtesy of our friend Greg Cleary — a great cake decorator.

Preparation: 15 minutes
Cooking: 5 minutes
Makes about 1.25 kg (2 lb 12 oz), enough to cover each cake in this book (with some left over in case of mishaps)

15 g (½ oz) powdered gelatine
125 ml (4 fl oz/½ cup) liquid glucose
25 ml (5 teaspoons) glycerine
1 kg (2 lb 4 oz) pure icing (confectioners') sugar
2 drops flavour extract (optional)

1 Sprinkle the gelatine over 60 ml (2 fl oz/¼ cup) water in a small heatproof bowl. Leave to stand for 3 minutes, or until the gelatine is spongy.
2 Place the bowl over a pan of simmering water and stir until the gelatine has dissolved. Add the glucose and glycerine and stir until melted. Strain through a fine sieve if the mixture is lumpy.
3 Sift the icing sugar into a large bowl. Make a well in the centre and pour in the warm gelatine mixture. Combine with a wooden spoon until it becomes too difficult to stir. Tip the mixture onto a bench, add the flavouring extract, if using, and knead with dry hands for 3–5 minutes, or until a smooth, pliable dough forms.
4 Wrap well in plastic wrap or in a zip-lock bag. Store in an airtight container in a cool place, but do not refrigerate.
5 Knead again before using, adding a little more sifted pure icing sugar if necessary.

FONDANT TIPS

- Fondant icing can dry out very quickly. It is important to work quickly so your icing doesn't become cracked and hard to use.
- Never use icing that is too dry or over-kneaded; this will make the icing on your cake crack very easily.
- NEVER EVER refrigerate icing when it is on a cake. Fondant will sweat in the fridge. Once a cake is covered, it should be stored in a cool place (about 20°C/68°F).
- Never ice cakes straight from the fridge. For a professional finish, always bring chilled cakes to room temperature before covering with icing.
- When not using your icing (even for a minute), put it in a good-quality zip-lock plastic bag to stop it drying out. Any excess or leftover icing is best stored the same way, or wrapped in plastic wrap and then in a sealed airtight container. Follow the manufacturer's instructions on how to store your particular brand of purchased icing. We store ours at room temperature.

- Hot hands may make your icing sticky. Don't be tempted to use too much cornflour (cornstarch), as it will dry the icing. Cool your hands under cold water and keep cornflour to a light sprinkle.
- Weather will also affect fondant icing. Humidity will make the icing sticky, and very cold weather will make it as hard as rock.
- Always work the icing in small amounts, and try to get above the icing when you knead it on the bench. If you are short, stand on a step stool so you can use your bodyweight to help you knead. If you try to knead large amounts of icing, you will put undue pressure on your wrists and make the job very difficult.
- Kneading icing is not like kneading dough: if you keep pummelling, it will stick to the board and become unmanageable. Treat icing a bit like Play-Doh, and keep folding it in until it is smooth and warm to use, but not sticking to the bench.
- To use fondant icing for modelling, knead 1 teaspoon Tylose powder into 450 g (1 lb) fondant until thoroughly combined.

Syrup

Preparation: 5 minutes
Cooking: none
Makes about 160 ml (5¼ fl oz)

115 g (4 oz/⅓ cup) apricot jam
2 teaspoons orange liqueur (optional)

1 Whisk the jam with 100 ml (3½ fl oz) boiling water until smooth.
2 Strain through a fine sieve to remove any lumps. Stir in the liqueur, if using.

Italian buttercream

This buttercream is best used immediately. The consistency should be smooth, and should be thick enough to hold its shape when piped. Test by running your finger over the frosting: it should hold its shape well, but not be stiff.

Preparation: 20 minutes
Cooking: 15 minutes
Makes 4 cups, enough to cover each cake in this book (with some left over in case of mishaps)

250 g (9 oz) caster (superfine) sugar
6 egg whites, at room temperature
375 g (13 oz) unsalted butter, just softened, chopped into walnut-sized pieces
1½ teaspoons vanilla extract

1 Put the sugar in a saucepan over low heat. Add 60 ml (2 fl oz/¼ cup) warm water and stir until the sugar has dissolved. Increase the heat to medium–high and bring to the boil. Allow to boil, without stirring, for 8–10 minutes, or until the syrup has thickened slightly, but isn't coloured — it should reach 110°C (225°F) on a sugar thermometer. Remove from the heat and stand briefly until the bubbles subside.
2 Meanwhile, beat the egg whites in a large bowl using electric beaters, until firm peaks form. Gradually beat in the hot sugar syrup on high speed until combined. Continue to beat for 8–10 minutes, or until the mixture has cooled to room temperature.
3 Gradually beat in the butter, one piece at a time, until combined — the frosting should be light and fluffy. Beat in the vanilla and use as desired.

TIP

Make sure the egg and sugar mixture has cooled to room temperature before adding the butter. If the mixture is too warm, the butter will melt, causing the frosting to split.

Vanilla buttercream

This buttercream is best used immediately. The consistency should be smooth, and should be thick enough to hold its shape when piped. Test by running your finger over the frosting: it should hold its shape well, but not be stiff. To adjust the consistency, if necessary, beat in a little more milk or icing sugar as needed.

Preparation: 10 minutes
Cooking: none
Makes 4 cups, enough to cover each cake in this book (with some left over in case of mishaps)

375 g (13 oz) unsalted butter, just softened
840 g (1 lb 13 oz/6¾ cups) soft icing (confectioners') sugar, sifted
80 ml (2½ fl oz/⅓ cup) milk
3 teaspoons vanilla extract

1 Beat the butter in a bowl using electric beaters for 5–6 minutes, or until it turns white.
2 Gradually beat in the icing sugar until smooth and creamy, scraping down the sides of the bowl as necessary.
3 Add the milk and vanilla and beat until well combined. Use as desired.

Royal icing

Achieving the right consistency for royal icing can be difficult. For piping with a piping bag and nozzle, you will need 'soft peak' royal icing — when lifted from the bowl with a spatula, the peak will stand up but droop over slightly at the tip, like uncooked meringue.

Preparation: 10 minutes
Cooking: none
Makes about 270 g (9½ oz/1 cup)

250–300 g (9–10½ oz/2–2½ cups) pure icing (confectioners') sugar, sifted
1 egg white
2–4 drops lemon juice or white vinegar

1 Put 250 g (9 oz/2 cups) of the icing sugar in a bowl with the egg white and lemon juice or vinegar. Beat with electric beaters on medium–high speed for 5 minutes for 'soft peaks' (less if you want it firmer). If the mixture becomes too soft, beat in a little more sifted icing sugar.
2 Store in an airtight container in a cool place, but do not refrigerate. The icing will keep for up to 4 days.

ICING TECHNIQUES

COLOURING FONDANT ICING

1 Measure the colour
Knead the icing to a pliable dough. Measure out a small amount of food colour (photo 1).

2 Add the colour
Smear the colour onto the icing (photo 2), then knead until it's evenly distributed. Wear gloves so your hands don't stain.

3 + 4 Check the colour
Cut through your icing to check if the colour is evenly blended (photo 3).

If there are still swirls of colour, keep kneading, and checking, until the colour is solid all the way through (photo 4).

Alternatively, leave the colour as it is for a marbled effect in your icing.

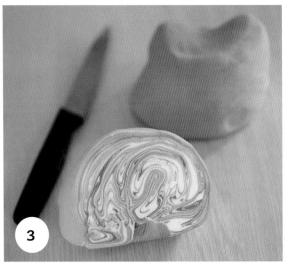

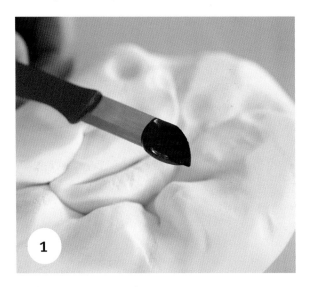

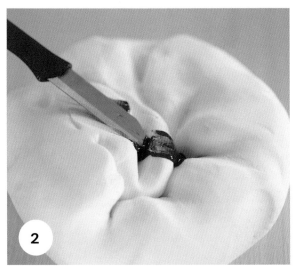

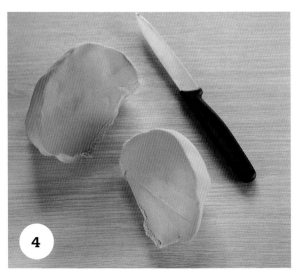

DEEP OR INTENSE COLOURS

When you want to colour your icing very strongly, making colours such as black, brown, red, orange, purple or royal blue, it's better to use paste food colour rather than liquid colour. To achieve these hues, you need to use much more colour, and using a liquid colour would make the icing too sticky to work with.

Even if you are using paste, colour your icing a day in advance, as it will be exceptionally soft due to the large amount of colour pigment, and the amount of kneading needed to thoroughly blend it in.

Standing the icing overnight will help firm it up, making it easier to work with.

COLOUR FADING

After the icing is coloured, you need to protect the colours from fading. Pinks, purples and blues are especially susceptible to fading out, even in a couple of hours. Pink and mauve can be reduced to almost white when exposed to sunlight; purples to blues; blues to grey.

Be careful to protect the icing from light, by covering your figurines with a cloth or keeping them in a cake box.

COLOURING FONDANT ICING FIGURINES

The important thing to remember when colouring icing for figurines is to add just a 'dot' of colour to the fondant, as you are colouring much smaller quantities of icing. Use a toothpick to add small dots of icing colour at a time.

You can also make more elaborate colours by mixing different icing colours together. We suggest using a colour wheel as a guide.

EDIBLE GLITTER

Non-toxic edible glitter is available from cake-decorating supply stores and is easy to apply.

Trace over the area where you wish to apply the glitter with a paintbrush coated with water, piping gel or sugar syrup.

Dust the wet area with edible glitter and wait until dry.

Dust away the excess glitter with a perfectly dry, soft brush.

GELLING

Translucent piping gel gives surfaces a shiny appearance. It can be used over coloured fondant, just as it comes, and on features such as eyes or noses, to make them look shiny and 'alive'.

Piping gel is also sometimes labelled as piping jelly and is available from cake-decorating stores.

Colouring paste can be added to the gel to achieve a depth of colour. We usually just brush it on with a pastry brush or paintbrush.

If you want a thick, even coating, pipe the gel onto the surface through a small piping nozzle, and smooth it with a palette knife if desired.

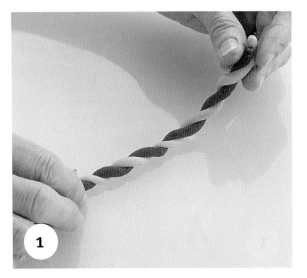

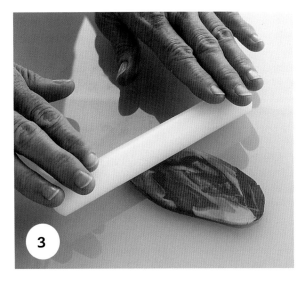

MARBLING

Marbling is a simple technique that creates an effective swirled pattern in the fondant.

1 Take two colours

Start with two small portions of fondant icing in different colours of your choice. Roll each portion into a rope, then twist them together (photo 1).

2 Roll into a ball

Roll the twisted rope into a ball in the palm of your hands (photo 2). Take care not to over-knead it or the colours will fuse into a single shade.

3 Roll out

Flatten the ball slightly (photo 3). Sprinkle your work surface with cornflour and roll out the fondant to the desired thickness.

4 Cut the icing

Cut out shapes (photo 4) and use as desired.

COVERING A BOARD WITH ICING

There are two methods of covering a cake board: to cover the whole board, or just to cover the part that is visible around the cake. It isn't necessary to cover the board at all — in fact many decorators don't.

I cover my boards because I like the clean finish it gives, and personally I don't like the look of silver or gold boards, which can undermine the effect of the cake.

Here's how to cover a whole cake board. If you use this method, it is essential that your cake sits on a set-up or temp board. For round and square cakes you can use ready-made boards as set-up boards.

1 Roll out the icing
Roll the icing to 3 mm (⅛ in) thick and at least the same size as the board. Place the icing on the board (photo 1). If it is too small, keep on rolling it directly on the board until it covers the whole surface.

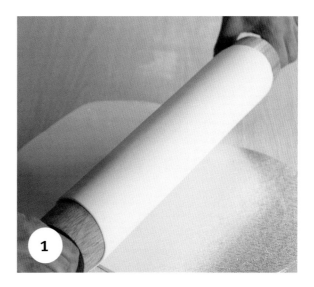

2 Make the icing stick
Dip a pastry brush in water. Lift the icing halfway up, brush the board with water and lay the icing down (photo 2); repeat on the other side.

3 Trim the icing
Run a flexi-scraper or an icing smoother over the surface to create a neat finish. Trim away most of the excess icing with scissors. Place the iced board on a turntable or halfway over the edge of the table. Hold the smoother at a 45° angle and slide it along the edge to cut the icing, to give a nice bevelled edge (photo 3).

Let the icing on the board dry, then stick the cake on it with a dab of royal icing (see page 177) to keep the cake on the board.

USING A PASTA MACHINE TO ROLL ICING

1 Roll out the icing with a rolling pin

Knead the icing, then roll it out using a small rolling pin (photo 1). Work out which setting on your pasta machine will roll pasta or icing to 3 mm (⅛ in) — this is the thickness we use for covering most cakes.

2 Run the icing through the pasta machine

Feed your piece of icing through the pasta machine, and keep feeding it through until it reaches a 3 mm (⅛ in) thickness, just as you would a piece of pasta (photo 2).

GLUING ICING

Always use a dab of water or gel to secure one piece of icing to another, even when you are also using dried spaghetti, a skewer or wire for support. Icing is made of sugar, so it will readily 'glue' to itself with water alone.

Make a very light line or dab of water or gel where the icing needs to be glued. Don't use too much — if you haven't applied enough water or gel, you can always add a little more, but if you apply too much, you may end up with a sodden mess.

Hold the icing piece in place for a few minutes, to see if it sets. A small, sharp utensil to hold and press together is useful for very small pieces or body parts.

You can also use a dab of royal icing (page 177), but it should be the same colour as the fondant it is being applied to, and used very sparingly.

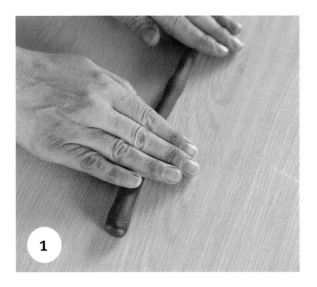

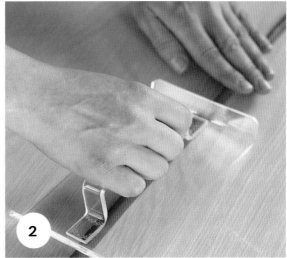

MAKING AN ICING ROLL

1 Roll the icing with your hands

Using your hands, roll the icing to the basic shape of a rope (photo 1, above).

2 Roll it even, using a smoother

Using an icing smoother, roll the rope back and forth, pulling it slightly out to the sides to elongate it (photo 2). If it slips, paint a thin line of water right next to and parallel to the rope, then use the smoother to roll the icing across the water. This will make the icing a little bit stickier, which will help it 'catch' and roll more easily.

Continue to roll and stretch the icing rope until it is the desired width and length.

TRACING A TEMPLATE ONTO A CAKE

1 Trace onto baking paper

Using a 2B pencil, trace your image onto baking paper. Turn the paper over and trace the back of the same image (photo 1, right).

2 Place it on the cake

Place the template right side up on the cake. Lightly shade the baking paper to transfer the image onto the cake (photo 2).

TROUBLE-SHOOTING

Working with fondant icing is generally quite simple, but every now and then little mishaps may occur. The good news, however, is that most little problems can be fixed. The techniques on the next few pages show how to deal with the issues that most commonly arise.

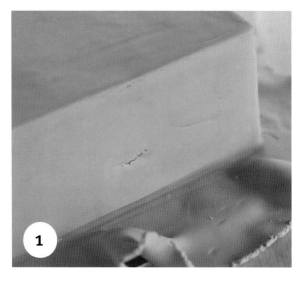

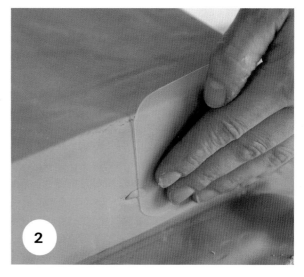

Mending torn icing

GAP IN ICING
Tearing is usually the result of smoothing and pulling your icing down too vigorously when covering the cake (see photo 1).

Smooth the tear
While the icing is still soft, use your hands and a flexi-scraper and massage the icing up and around the tear, so that the tear gap is closed and almost invisible (photo 2).

If you are still left with a hole, wait until the icing has dried (next day).

Make a small ball of fresh icing in the same colour as your base, then massage the fresh icing into the tear, like putty. Smooth the icing with a flexi-scraper and allow to dry.

Covering up cracked icing

Cracks usually appear on corners or edges of the cake when the icing is too dry.

A huge crack is impossible to fix — but you can cover it up with some decorations, such as icing flowers, so nobody will notice it!

Mending cracked icing

While your icing is still soft, use very warm hands and massage the icing inwards around the cracks, closing them and rendering them almost invisible.

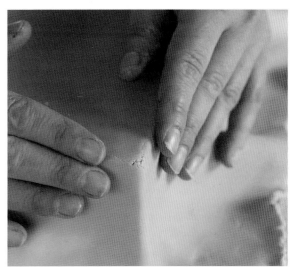

Air bubbles

Always try to eliminate air bubbles under your icing, as they will get bigger and lift the icing off the cake.

Feel over your cake for any air bubbles, then lightly prick any with a pin to let the air escape. Smooth over your icing using a flexi-scraper.

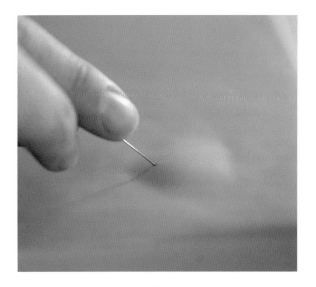

Cleaning stained icing

CORNFLOUR STAIN
1 Apply decorating alcohol
Apply decorating alcohol on the stain with a soft paintbrush (photo 1, below). The alcohol will absorb the cornflour.

2 Pat dry
Pat the spot dry with a soft tissue (photo 2).

CHOCOLATE STAIN
1 Wash with soapy water
Using a soft paintbrush, lightly wash the stain with a very small amount of warm soapy water.

2 Dust with cornflour
Rinse your brush and wash the soap away with clean water. Lightly dry the area with a tissue (photo 1, below), then lightly dust with cornflour using a soft brush (photo 2, below).

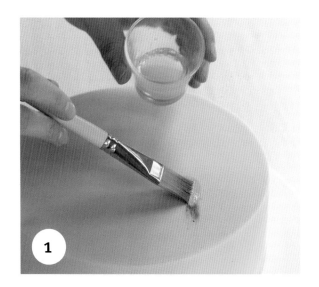

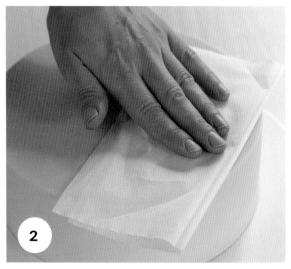

Humidity

Due to humidity, icing often becomes soft and sticky. To solve this, mix sifted icing (confectioners') sugar into the icing a little at a time and knead it through.

Icing too dry

If your icing is dry and cracking, apply a little water to it, using a brush, then knead it through.

Alternatively, brush the icing with a small amount of glycerine (see Glossary, page 171) and knead it through.

Icing too wet

Wet icing is usually the result of too much colour pigment. This is why black, red and brown icing often becomes 'wet' and difficult to work with.

To solve this, knead some sifted icing (confectioners') sugar into your icing a little at a time, until it becomes less sticky but is still pliable.

INDEX